tuscan living

From the Yorkshire Moors to the Tuscan Hills

tuscan living

From the Yorkshire Moors to the Tuscan Hills

Sarah Fraser

Photography by Ben Duffy

CASSELL ILLUSTRATED

First published in 2003 by Cassell Illustrated,
a division of Octopus Publishing Group Limited,
2–4 Heron Quays, London E14 4JP

Text © 2003 Sarah Fraser
Photographs © 2003 Kirsty Gibson

A CIP catalogue record for this book is available from the British Library.

ISBN 1 84403 182 9

Photography: Ben Duffy
Art Direction and Design: Emma George
Managing Editor: Anna Cheifetz
Project Manager: Kirsty Gibson
Printed in Great Britain by Bath Press

Contents

Introduction

Richard and I are 'ordinary' people. In Yorkshire we lived in a small house and didn't have much money to spare. We worked hard and looked after our young son Gregory. I'm still amazed that our dreams have actually become a reality, but our move to Tuscany confirms that life really is a long list of opportunities just waiting to be discovered.

The first thing that everyone said when we told them our plans was, 'You're doing what! But why?', closely followed by either, 'You're mad,' or a very dubious, 'Wow, good luck'. Richard and I have also been called 'brave' and even 'stupid' in the past, but the decision to move was more the culmination of a number of factors.

Richard and I both love challenges. We've always bought houses in dire need of repair and even lived in a two-berth caravan while we renovated our last home in Yorkshire. I was seven months pregnant with Gregory at the time. We both feel that you should push yourself in whatever you do and running our own businesses has given us a certain amount of self-belief and motivation.

We're also terribly impulsive, so buying a house off the internet and moving country within 14 weeks was not too outlandish for us. I proposed to Richard only 15 days after we met in 1996 and we've rarely been parted since. The life-changing decision to move abroad seemed relatively well thought out by comparison.

Finally, three years ago we were made very aware that you should live life to full when I was diagnosed with cervical cancer. I'd just given birth to Gregory and we couldn't believe that I might now face death. Fortunately I had an operation straight away and subsequent checks have all been clear. We were lucky enough to be able to turn this dreadful experience into something positive; we now take nothing for granted, we seize every opportunity offered to us, and we know that no amount of money can buy happiness.

It seemed we were ripe for the move to the most beautiful and joyful of countries – *bella Italia.* This book is a record of the trials and triumphs we experienced along the way, including some handy advice and invaluable recipes. I hope you enjoy the read and if we in any way inspire you to do something you've only dreamed of then we consider ourselves honoured.

Sarah x

From Yorkshire

Richard and I grew up in the shadow of the Cow and Calf Rocks on Ilkley Moor, we met in Ilkley, married in Leeds and lived in Otley – all within a 10-mile radius. We only thought about moving abroad in the same way that everyone dreams of 'leaving it all behind' – no basis in reality. Yet that is exactly what we did and we've learnt that 'reality' can be whatever you want.

When you've lived in a place all your life it is part of you and, inevitably, you begin to take it for granted. Moving to Tuscany has allowed us to rediscover our roots while embarking on the greatest adventure of our lives.

Our roots

Yorkshire is beautiful; I love the dark brooding mass of hills around Otley Chevin and the smell of the air, washed clean after a storm. The land is hilly and lush, rivers run everywhere (often onto roads when it rains a lot) and copses and woods break the wildness of the moors.

Being close to nature has always been important to us. We spent many weekends camping by rivers, enjoying the total night darkness of the countryside, walking the hills and visiting favourite villages for a hearty lunch or afternoon tea.

Away from the moors, the rolling fields near our house were given over to dairy and sheep farming. Ancient dry-stone walls cut through the landscape, patching it together. There is little livestock in the part of Tuscany where we live now and the hills are dissected by olive groves and vineyards, but the flowing line of valleys, the country ways and wildness are all important links with what we've left behind.

We spent many weekends walking the bracken-covered hills of Ilkley Moor, near our West Yorkshire home.

Summer 2000

The year had been dismal in England, with foot and mouth disease turning the countryside into a graveyard. As a family we loved camping in the Dales and the Lake District and walking the dogs on the moors near our home. Another passion was striking out on my horse, Bojangles, exploring the hills and country lanes. All this stopped with the outbreak of foot and mouth disease. We couldn't take the dogs anywhere off the leash and horses were kept stabled so as not to spread the disease to neighbouring farms. The news was, quite rightly, doom and gloom, with suicides among farmers and the countryside in crisis.

As spirits flagged, the Government encouraged us to visit rural areas and spend our money in the floundering tourist attractions, but in reality this was impossible. The countryside was effectively out of bounds as farmers, understandably, didn't want visitors spreading disease on car tyres and shoes. Confined to the house, we were all miserable.

The months dragged on and we longed to escape from the fog of depression that hung over Yorkshire. In late summer 2000, I was shopping in our local supermarket when I spied an advert for a Tuscan holiday villa on the noticeboard. Later, at home, I looked it up on the internet and showed Richard. It looked fantastic. I'd only visited Italy once on a school skiing trip, but Richard had been twice and loved the place. He expounded at length on the friendliness of the people, the beauty of the landscape and Italy's amazing history. The last point I took with a pinch of salt, as Richard is usually as culturally aware as, well, someone who isn't. He used to tease me about my history degree, saying, 'It's all in the past – what good is it going to do you?'. Still, he loved Italy and we needed a holiday so what better way to cheer ourselves up than a jaunt to Tuscany? The end of summer arrived and we didn't get away.

The outbreak of foot and mouth disease meant that the fields and moorland near our home were off limits.

Richard's impressive Jimmy Savile impersonation was used for popular 1970s theme nights and charity events.

Work, work, work

At this time, Richard was running a successful disco business, and I had started my own corporate hospitality firm with a friend. We were so busy that neither of us felt we could take a holiday. In retrospect, this was the beginning of our troubles; when you can't find time for each other, then you are heading for problems.

Richard worked at least four nights a week and much of the weekend either DJing at weddings, or running children's parties. Part of the fun was a frighteningly good impersonation of Jimmy Savile, which he performed at charity dinners and 1970s theme nights. On days off, he worked on improving the house and looking after our young son Gregory.

I worked an ordinary week, nine to five, and also helped on weekends with the discos. Gregory went to nursery almost full time. It was a hard grind, with long, unsociable hours but we were 'on the up' and didn't notice the cracks beginning to appear in our relationship.

There was no longer time to enjoy family camping trips, days out or even walking the dogs together. I was probably more to blame for this than Richard. My office was based in our conservatory, so work intruded constantly into home life. Even when I took a day off, my business partner Rachel would be in the office next to our kitchen and I would be drawn into something to do with work. I constantly shouted at Gregory to be quiet because we had important telephone calls to make and quiet is not a natural state for a three-year-old boy in his own home.

Work pressures combined with suffering cervical cancer just after Gregory's birth meant that life felt short. I put myself under increasing pressure to do everything and to do it right now – wife, mother, bread-winner, cook and gardener. Instead of being a success I was grumpy and unreasonable.

September 11th 2001

We saw the wreck of the first tower smoking. Then watched in horror as the second was destroyed.

Inexplicable, dreadful and incomprehensible. Satellites beamed us images of people jumping from windows as the towers collapsed. Previously, I had focused on all the things I wanted to acquire or achieve in the future. It suddenly seemed far more important to concentrate on the value of now. What was the point of all my materialism? Who would I have rung if I'd been on one of those planes? It certainly wasn't the office, so why wasn't I spending more time with my family?

Shortly afterwards I was driving home from an appointment in Northumberland. It was a four-hour journey, it was raining (no surprise) and I was stuck in a traffic jam. It was a life-changing moment. As I sat staring at the blurred bumper in front of me I thought, 'If I only worked a little more, I'd earn more money and could pay a nanny so I wouldn't have to drive home in this bad weather – I could have stayed at the hotel I've just visited'. I turned the thought over; it was just about possible. Then, slowly, like the mist rising on the road before me, I realised the warped logic of my plans. I wanted to work harder and longer so that someone else could raise my child.

No wonder Richard said I'd changed, I had, and I was disgusted with myself. For the rest of the journey I wondered how I'd lost my way. I could list the reasons but really they were just excuses. I'd simply got on the treadmill and not realised that the faster you run, the faster you have to go and the more personal sacrifices you have to make. The decision to change my lifestyle – the first stage in deciding to move abroad – had happened.

The disco business required long, unsociable hours and weekend work. We had little time for family life.

Desperate for a warm winter holiday, an Italian internet site provided a source of rental villas in Tuscany.

Loosening ties: Winter 2002

So, what to do next? First, I reduced my hours in the business by half. Next was Operation Happy Family. We had already booked a cottage in Hertford for a few days' break, but I thought we should also go some-where warmer in the New Year. Tuscany sprang straight to mind. I logged back on to the Italian internet site and looked at the rental villas. On the site there was also a real estate section. I entered, as you do, to have a peek at the lovely houses I'd never live in. There were some real beauties. Spacious villas with incredible views and azure pools. Small hill town apartments, fabulously renovated, overlooking quaint piazzas. And then there was Casa del Sole. An eighteenth century farmhouse with 15 acres of olive groves and woodland, it was perfect in every way. Well, to me at least; it was in a terrible state.

I called Richard to have a look. I wanted him to see my dream house. I must admit that at this point I had no idea of its cost as I didn't even know the value of a euro. In fact, even if I had known the value of a euro I'd still have had difficulties doing the maths. Richard scrolled through the pictures of the house, the view, the olive trees. He noted the lack of bathroom, something I seemed to have overlooked. But what the heck, 'if you live in paradise, you probably don't need a bathroom,' I said, only half joking – I was in love.

'Well,' I said, 'What do you think?' The unexpected reply was 'We could just about afford it. Email and see if we can have a look.' 'What?' I spluttered, 'You're not serious? You can't go all the way to Italy just to look at a house that you're not going to buy.' 'Why not?' he asked seriously. Although on reflection he did have that smug, 'I'm going to say something to really blow you away' look on his face. 'Because,' I replied, appalled that he could toy with my emotions like this, 'it's bad manners to pretend you're interested in buying a house just so you can have a look around. And anyway, you know I hate window shopping.' Richard looked pointedly at the computer screen. 'But that's different, I was only looking,' I said, realising I'd been caught out. Richard continued swiftly before I had chance to get cross with him, 'No, what I meant was, why can't we buy it?'

Cold February dreams

The thing with Richard is that he has lots of ideas, millions of them. Some are really good and some ridiculous. Sometimes he believes in what he is saying and sometimes he is just fantasising. This idea was so far-fetched that I didn't really believe him, but I went along with it anyway because I adored the house and because everyone should be allowed to dream.

I emailed the property's owner asking for details. Then, at great and tedious length, I converted the euro price into sterling – £110,000 – not out of our league, but that was before the cost of moving and renovation, solicitors' fees, tax and anything else that might crop up. I decided to think about that later. After all, we were just looking…

We waited and waited for a reply, but none came. I emailed the owner again. In the meantime we went on holiday to Hertford. It rained, a lot. We shouldn't have expected anything less in England in February, but we were caught in some of the largest floods in that area for a century. Still, we didn't mind; the point of the holiday was to spend time together and discuss the future.

Among the lists of expensive villas and apartments was Casa del Sole, a dilapidated olive farm in Tuscany.

Making plans

I decided that the only way to gain more family time was to sell my business. With this major issue agreed, I broached the subject of Casa del Sole. The beautiful old monastery where we were staying in Hertford had a bar selling perry – a potent cider made from pears. Plying Richard with a couple of pints, I asked whether he was serious about the house. I needn't have bothered with the perry as he rushed to explain how we could manage it. The details were a bit sketchy but he confessed that he was desperate to move abroad and that Italy was the place for him. He was willing to either sell the disco business or run it through a manager. Simple. We'd just sell up and move on out.

This was real excitement. Now I'd decided to leave my work partnership there was nothing holding me in Yorkshire. My family is small and scattered, so I had few qualms about moving abroad on those grounds. Richard's unsociable hours and punishing workload also meant that we wouldn't be deserting a busy social life. It wasn't as though we were moving to Australia – flights to Europe were cheap and friends and family could easily visit. We returned from our wet week away very happy and full of ideas.

As soon as we got home I raced to the computer and downloaded our emails. A reply from Casa del Sole at last. A deep breath and suddenly all our dreams were stilled. The house was sold, subject to contract. I was utterly deflated.

Right Our small semi-detached house in Otley had few rooms and a tiny yard at the back. Below Otley, West Yorkshire.

Our options

Richard was not going to be put off by such a setback. As soon as he'd had dinner (always the most important thing for Richard), he sat down and began surfing the internet for other properties. Watching Richard use the computer is like watching a dog chewing a wasp. It's a painful, longwinded process and there's a lot of face-pulling involved. Really it would be kinder to take the mouse from him but, for some reason, he enjoys it. Eventually he was happy that he'd found all he could on the subject. It seemed we just couldn't afford most of the property for sale in Italy. The advertised houses were targeting buyers who wanted expensive holiday lets, not basic homes. Still, there were a few of interest, mostly in Tuscany, so I emailed for more information.

Attempting to widen our options I suggested France as an alternative. After all, I could already speak a bit of French and a diet of croissants certainly held some appeal. (Neither of us had mastered any Italian.) We started looking around the south of France and found that prices were a lot more reasonable. Still, Richard wasn't completely convinced. His dream was Italy, so Italy it had to be – and the dream must have been pretty vivid to overcome the economics. I didn't mind where we went; it was the challenge and adventure that was intriguing me.

From plans to action

Wherever we ended up, our plans were certainly pulling us away from Yorkshire. It was time to sell up and try something new. Leaving the sale of my company to my business partner Rachel, I concentrated on trying to find a buyer for our home. We were extremely lucky; the house market couldn't have been stronger. We got a good valuation and put the house up for sale immediately. Unbelievably, it was sold within days.

The Cow and Calf Rocks rise above the broad sweep of Ilkley Moor, near where Richard and I grew up.

From Yorkshire

SEARCHING FOR OUR PERFECT HOUSE

Casa del Sole seemed out of our grasp, but Italy had captured our imagination. In spring, we finally headed for the sunny Tuscan hills and began the search for our dream house.

Tiny hill towns and villages perch on the mountainsides of the Garfagnana region in northern Tuscany.

Spring 2002

We decided to go and have a look at some of the properties in Italy that Richard had found on the internet. We went to book the flights and were amazed at their low cost. This changed our plans slightly. If Richard could travel back and forth from Italy cheaply, he could keep his disco business running as a safety net. He could manage the company from Italy, just commuting to Yorkshire every few weeks to keep it on track. With a guaranteed, regular income we could take out a mortgage immediately and easily afford some of the houses we'd seen. Everything seemed to be falling into place.

Into the Garfagnana

We travelled to northern Tuscany in the first week of March and stayed in a cottage in the village of Benabbio, in the Garfagnana region. The twisting mountain roads filled with nausea-inducing bumps made the rental car ride a spectacle of raised voices, flung maps and missed

turnings. Finally, winding up a steep mountainside we emerged stunned into a tiny village. Perched, seemingly in the middle of nowhere, was a thriving community with shops, a church, bar and large number of residents. Welcome to the phenomenon of the Tuscan hill town. Just when you thought that the road was too narrow, too rocky, or a little too far from civilisation, hey presto! Around the next turn sits a bustling centre, completely self-absorbed in its day-to-day business.

Benabbio was beautiful with spectacular views. Our cottage was basic, but to us (perhaps naively) charmingly rustic and gave us a good idea of what we might expect from some of the properties in the area.

In the evenings we were treated to a soft peach sunset over the surrounding mountains. In the mornings, the mist lay in the valley far below us; we were on a wooded island floating in the clouds. The early light was cold and brilliant on the hilltops, picking out villages on the opposite side of the valley. If we could have sailed to them, they would have been only a couple of miles away. In reality, zigzagging on mountain roads, it would have taken an hour at least to reach them by car. The landscape was breathtaking and romantic; I fell in love with Italy too.

The first properties we viewed were in the remote mountain villages of northern Tuscany.

The mountains offered splendid isolation and spectacular scenery, but few facilities for our new life.

Mountain life

The Garfagnana area falls within a national park. In England its equivalent would be the Lake District. The countryside is craggy and majestic, the towns are quaint and interesting. Apart from tourism, there is little industry. It's a wonderful place to visit but I realised very quickly that I couldn't live there. We would have been too far from an airport and I didn't want to be isolated on an inaccessible mountainside. A great area to retire to perhaps, but I wanted a more integral part in Italian life – to be closer to a town, to be near a hospital, facilities for Gregory, work opportunities, the list went on.

The estate agents were also a deterrent. We had organised to visit 13 houses in our short stay but found that agents just didn't understand our intention to live in Italy full time. At the start of each viewing the agent would show us, with expansive flourish, where we could build the swimming pool. We would explain that this wasn't a priority; they would patiently counter that we would double our rental value by installing one. We'd repeat that we intended to live in the house, not rent it out. The confused agent would move on to explain how restoration would increase the property's resale value. True, we'd concede, but this was of little importance as we weren't buying to sell on. At this point we lost any credence as buyers. The agent would take us to the next property in his portfolio and have the same conversation all over again, probably hoping that he'd frightened some sense into us on the precipitous mountain roads.

The final black mark against the Garfagnana came when an agent proudly described how he'd sold all the houses on a hillside (some twice over) to British buyers. We wanted to move to Italy to escape the UK; we wanted to get to know Italian people, experience the way of life, the food. The plan was to integrate as far as possible, not to join an established ex-pat community in the sun.

In the Garfagnana, we would spend winter up a mountain with few neighbours and spend summer crowded by holidaymakers. This was not the dream. To be fair, most of the estate agents were extremely helpful; we were obviously just looking in the wrong place for our perfect home.

A last look

I began to panic about whether we would ever find the right sort of house in the right location. Scolding myself, I tried to focus on the fact that this was only our first house-hunting trip; I should calm down, look harder and not expect miracles. We had one day left and, despite seeing some lovely properties, nothing had captivated us.

My thoughts drifted constantly to Casa del Sole. Couldn't we just go and have a look at the area, slightly to the south, to see if it was more suitable? I nagged Richard, 'Please just ring to ask if we could look at the house. You never know, it might be back on the market.'

After much arm twisting, he rang. Christian, the owner, was German but fortunately spoke good English. He was surprised to hear from us, and even more surprised when he learned that we were in Italy and wondering whether his sale had gone through. If we'd known a little more about Italian bureaucracy at this stage, we needn't have asked. He told Richard that just the day before, the sale had fallen through; we could go and see the house.

Not for the first time since I met Richard I found myself wondering how I could be this lucky. I was jittery with excitement – this was the house, I just knew it. Not because of the grainy pictures I'd seen on the internet. Not because on paper it sounded ideal – I'd worked for an estate agent and knew the score. But because my heart told me so. I just knew it.

Left and below Many classic stone houses were available for restoration, but most were out of our price range.

Into the sun

We drove down out of the mountains towards Pescia. Six miles from Casa del Sole, this was the nearest town. The countryside mellowed, becoming less austere and more like my preconceptions of 'real' Tuscany. Sweeping hills, olive terraces and vineyards descended to valleys and streams.

We found the town easily, being of a fair size and with good road connections. The hub of Italy's cut flower business, it sat in a flat plain, surrounded by broad sweeping flower fields and peppered with greenhouses. We made our way to the shuttered, historic centre and to the bar where we were to meet Christian, the owner of the house.

We were late, but he'd waited. Draining an espresso, he asked us to follow and set off at incredible speed in a tiny Fiat Panda. Richard launched into 'racing driver' mode to follow, while I screwed my eyes shut (I still shut my eyes sometimes, even when I'm the driver).

We drove through cobbled streets, over a lazy river and along a narrow road into the hills. All of a sudden the little car in front swung left up a small track. Taking sharp intakes of breath, we turned forwards and back along hairpin bends. Finally, the Fiat stopped and I looked around expectantly for the house. Trees rose thickly on either side of the road. Christian explained that the driveway had not been finished so we'd have to continue on foot. The house was only two minutes away he assured us. Ten passed and we stopped to pant on the steep path. At least I'd get fit, I reasoned. Carrying a small child plus the shopping up a calf-straining slope every day would surely be good exercise.

Below We easily found Pescia, the nearest town to Casa del Sole, only a few miles away. Right The Pescia river dissects the town's medieval layout.

Casa del Sole

We came at the house from the side. The afternoon sun hit the long building, colouring the stonework pale gold. Basking in the warmth, the house asserted itself as though it had been there forever, a solid part of the hillside, part of the culture; home.

Home, but a home in complete disarray. The building was crumbling, the land a mass of overgrown grass and weeds. But I'd seen enough farms to know that they were rarely tidy. I looked beyond the confusion of corrugated plastic and broken machinery and was filled with excitement. Serious work was needed. The house had no bathroom or toilet. No boiler, so no hot water. The downstairs rooms comprised stables and outdoor storage. The roof sagged with holes. Windows, doors, floors, beams, all needed replacing. There was no access road. And then, there were the olives – 350 trees to tend and 15 acres to care for. To many people the house would have been a white elephant to be avoided at all costs. We knew that we had to have it.

The offer: April 2002

We sat down on a dusty wall and told Christian we wanted the house. Offering the full asking price, we were confident that it would be ours. I held my breath. Christian explained that while he'd love to accept, he had already promised a lady from Hong Kong that she could view the house. She was due at Easter, three weeks away. Calmly Richard asked if a higher offer would seal the sale. But still the answer was 'No', Christian couldn't go back on his word to the lady. There was nothing to do but return to Yorkshire and wait. Frustrated and bemused, we walked back down the driveway to the car. Neither of us said anything but I couldn't help shedding a few silent tears.

We travelled home, convinced that Casa del Sole was our perfect home but fearful it would slip away from us again. All we could do was complete the sale of our house in Otley and hope for the best.

After three agonising weeks, Christian rang on Good Friday to say that the house was ours. Yet again I marvelled at providence. Richard travelled out to Italy alone in mid-April to sign the preliminary contract on Casa del Sole. That was it, there was no going back.

May 2002

We were due to leave England on the 26th of May. The whole decision-making process and organisation of a complete lifestyle change had taken less than four months. We certainly hadn't dragged our feet.

Casa del Sole sits on a hillside above Pescia. Surrounded by ancient woodland and olive groves, it has sweeping views of the neighbouring valleys.

Learning from our experience

PLANNING OUR MOVE

Leaving Yorkshire for Tuscany involved a major lifestyle change. When planning our big move we carefully considered a number of factors, but there were many that we hadn't thought through.

What we knew

- We wanted to take control and change our way of life.

- We both wanted to leave the country.

- We both wanted to build the same sort of lifestyle – to be more self-sufficient, to spend more time together, to find a new way of working.

- We are both quite adventurous. This kind of mission is exciting and full of risks, but we were ready for the challenge. There were no guarantees that we would be able to support ourselves and we expected the move would place our relationship under pressure, even if our plans worked in the end.

- Our practical circumstances allowed us to move. We were self-employed, we had sold our house, we had no pressing ties or obligations at home.

- The timing was right. We are action people and realised that if we wanted to change our lives, we had to do it now – it was no good saying 'Oh well, maybe next year'. It might be too late.

- There are plenty of cheap flights from Italy to the UK so we could always visit family and friends and they could visit us.

- As Italy is an EU country we would be able to obtain residency and work.

- We were financially able to move. Savings and our house sale provided immediate funds for a new home. The possibility of Richard continuing to work in the UK was a financial safety net for day-to-day support and mortgage repayments.

What we hadn't considered

- We would be together ALL THE TIME. Richard likes this; it drives me a bit nuts sometimes. But we do love each other's company and being alone together for long stretches is no hardship. Tuscany has proved that we could probably survive if we were cast away on a desert island with no one else for company.

- Taking language lessons as a family before we left would have saved a lot of confusion and allowed us to integrate more quickly.

- We hadn't properly considered the climate of our new location. Holidaying in the sun is not the same as having to work in 40°C heat. The first summer in Tuscany was unbearably hot and the winter was unexpectedly wet. Some extra research would have prepared us.

- The real cost of moving is always far greater than the estimated cost.

- Financial and personal administration always takes more time than you expect – factor in sufficient time for closing bank accounts, cancelling direct debits, organising utilities readings and, of course, packing.

- You may be able to continue your pension contributions if you retain a bank or building society account in the UK. We reduced our contributions but as Richard was still working part-time in England we decided to maintain our English accounts and he continued his fund.

- If you are taking pets, research the regulations in your destination country and any countries that you will pass through. France and Italy have more stringent regulations than the UK and our dogs required additional vaccinations to travel.

- We decided to move our belongings ourselves. This saved funds but meant we had to rely on friends and family to help us with packing and storage.

- Buying an Italian SIM card for our mobile phones would have saved us money on telephone calls.

The House

We had found our dream house – Casa del Sole – a tumble-down olive farm in the gentle hills between Pisa and Lucca. Now we had to make it ours. It can take months to progress through the mire of paperwork from initial contract to proud ownership.

First, you make your offer. Then the nail-biting wait. If accepted, you sign a compromesso (preliminary contract) and pay your deposit. The bureaucracy begins. Finally you pay the balance and the house becomes yours.

Richard travelled alone to Italy in April to sign the initial contract. We moved in May. It was to take a further frustrating six months before the farm was truly ours. At last in November we started renovating our dream home.

Buying our house in the sun

Purchasing a house in Italy is very different to buying in the UK. Once your offer is accepted, you sign a *compromesso* (preliminary contract). This records the details of the house and adjoining land, specifies what you've agreed to pay, the amount of your deposit (usually around 30 per cent) and when you will pay the balance – at which point the house becomes yours.

If you pull out of the sale after signing the *compromesso* you lose your deposit. If the vendors pull out, they must pay you double the deposit amount. While the sale isn't complete, it is therefore very unlikely to fall through after this point. This means that in Italy it is common to move into a house that you don't yet own. This was how we found ourselves at Casa del Sole in May after signing a *compromesso* in April.

The average time lapse from first to final contract and completion is about six months, but you can agree any amount of time with the vendor. One of our neighbours took three years to complete, during which time they lived in the property and paid off the vendor in instalments. Flexibility seems to be the order of the day, as with many things in Italy.

Christian, our German vendor, was feeling less Italian about our sale. He would allow us to move into our dream home, but was less keen for us to begin any renovations until the final contract was complete.

Rather than take unnecessary items, we used relocation as a good excuse to ruthlessly pare down our possessions.

We didn't know this while we were negotiating the sale, so I bumbled along believing that any day now we would sign the final contract and could start on my priority – installing a water system and a bathroom.

In fact it was to take a further six months for us to finalise the paperwork and 10 months to gain a functioning toilet. In the meantime, we started loosening the ties of our old life in Yorkshire, packing our bags and preparing for the big move.

Packing our bags

Our last three weeks in England were chaotic. I was preoccupied with transferring my business to its new owner (more a case of dumping it in her lap and running). Life was a whirlwind of packing, making travel bookings, organising finances and documents and having leaving dinners with friends. We had no time to feel nervous or to worry about the consequences of leaving Yorkshire – probably one of the factors that made the move easier. Gregory understood that we were moving house, but equally had no concept of the further implications on his life.

Organising the move of our dogs was our biggest headache. We'd planned to drive to Tuscany through France, and French vaccination laws are particularly stringent. Pets must be vaccinated against rabies three weeks before entering the country. We were due to travel in just two – the move would have to be delayed by a week. In retrospect this was probably no bad thing – we hadn't even finished packing at this stage.

I was merciless in redistributing all our unnecessary possessions. Gregory, I realised, had more toys than he could have played with in three childhoods. The local charity shops must have wondered how one household could offload so many belongings. In the end I was amazed that three people could actually pare down their worldly goods to fit into a small VW van and trailer. I even managed to smuggle in a few of my favourite books when Richard wasn't looking.

We planned to take our dogs with us. In order to travel through France and Italy, they needed extra vaccinations.

Moving on

We had decided to move ourselves. This was primarily a money-saving measure, but there was also something appealingly final about trekking across Europe to our new home. We were embarking on our biggest adventure yet and it was indescribably exciting.

Richard's disco van and trailer were requisitioned for the move. Turntables, lights and the nylon tracksuits were replaced by crockery, essential furniture and the dogs. My mum had agreed to fly Gregory to Italy in a couple of days. At least this meant we didn't have to fit all our belongings, a small child, two dogs and two grumpy adults in the confined space of the van.

The rain hammered on the windows of our old house as we tucked Gregory up in bed for the last time. He didn't understand that we were moving to Italy, but he was certainly excited to be going on an aeroplane with Grandma. I was glad that he wasn't any older – it would have been a terrible wrench to make him leave established friends and school behind.

We left Gregory behind in England while we drove our belongings across Europe. He would follow two days later.

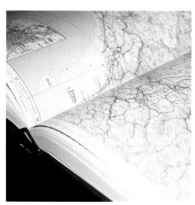

26th May 2002

We set off at around 2am and shared the driving down to Dover. One of us slept for three hours perched on our (now impractical) cream sofa in the back of the van while the other drove. The ferry crossing was easy and, at less than an hour, much shorter than I'd imagined. We found ourselves looking out of the front of the ferry to the future rather than waving goodbye to the English cliffs behind. It was raining; Italy beckoned.

On the boat, we just had time to eat the best cooked breakfast I'd ever tasted and we were on the road again. It continued to rain as we travelled on through France. The landscape, flat and greyed by the weather, seemed lifeless. I was glad that Richard had talked me out of moving here.

Late at night we'd made it to the Frejus Tunnel on the Italian border. A relief at last from the drowning, rain-soaked roads. It was early morning when we emerged on the Italian side; miraculously, it had stopped raining. This was a good omen and, after 20 hours pulling a trailer through the spray, we needed cheering up.

South to the sun

The scenery was breathtaking as we drove south. Approaching Genoa, the mountains reached right out to the sparkling sea, ridges and steep cliffs turning the coast into a folding mass of green.

The *autostrada* skims along the coast here, cutting sharply into the hillside when a mass of land gets in its way. Countless tunnels and bridges whisk you along this most spectacular route. Negotiating winding roads without the benefit of Italian driving skills, we only stole glimpses of the beauty around us, concentrating more on keeping our heart rates below critical.

Just before Genoa we sped from a tunnel onto an impossibly high bridge. Stretching out over the bustling city and back into the cliff face beyond, the two narrow lanes didn't feel adequate to hold so much traffic. Trucks whizzed past and our trailer wobbled precariously in their slipstream. I panicked while Richard snored through the whole ordeal. Moving to Italy was certainly going to require a new set of driving skills.

Rolling hills and pretty medieval towns provided spectacular scenery on our drive south through Italy.

Home

We had been travelling for 26 hours with only quick naps in service areas but were far too excited to feel tired. Speeding down the mountainside towards our new life, the trailer bumped along the highway behind us.

Finally at 11.30am we arrived back at Pescia, our local market town. Nudging the foot of the mountains in northern Tuscany, it is caught in a fortuitous triangle between ski resort (Abetone), culture (Florence and Pisa) and the seaside (Viareggio). We made our way through the cobbled main square as the sun shone on the plaster-fronted buildings; pale pink, crumbling ochre and white. Everything was as beautiful as I remembered from our previous visit in March.

Winding our way up the narrow track I marvelled at how far spring had advanced here. It was now May and the land was lush and green, magnificently wild. As we approached the house I had a strong sense of arriving home. There were wild strawberries along the path and countless flowers bobbed on the grassy olive terraces. An old blue cartwheel had been nailed to the yellow walls of the house. There was a lot of work to be done but we couldn't wait to start. This was the first sight of our new Italian home, business and life.

Left and right We arrived back among the shuttered houses and cobbled streets of Pescia, our local market town.

The House

CASA DEL SOLE

The main building at the property is the farmhouse. Sturdy and reassuring, the structure is typical of this part of Tuscany. It was built out of local stone, actually quarried on our land, around 1790.

Off to the left of the gravel track, the house nestles into the steep hillside. Like all traditional Tuscan buildings, the yellow stone walls have no foundations. At their bases, the walls are stout and at least two feet thick, reducing slightly as they get higher.

Windows are small to resist the searing heat of summer and prevent precious warmth escaping in winter. Even on the hottest of days, the hand-made bricks of the terracotta floors feel beautifully cool underfoot. As with the other houses dotting the hillsides with red, terracotta tiles

have also been used on the roof. This is supported by chestnut beams which reach darkly across the ceilings.

The day-to-day living space was located upstairs in the farmhouse and comprised four large bedrooms, an outdoor *loggia* (balcony) a kitchen and lounge. Downstairs were two large *cantinas* (storerooms), one of which had been used to house animals, and a storage area. The toilet and shower – a dribble from a clogged head – were located in a rickety wooden shed in the garden and looked out over the valley. More promising, and also outside, were a brick pizza oven and a small stone house built for roasting chestnuts.

Far left and above Built in traditional style, Casa del Sole has small windows and doors. Left The chestnut house.

The farm

Casa del Sole was built as an olive farm. The deeds state this but it is also obvious from the land – the steep hillside makes it hard to grow anything else. And even olive cultivation is difficult. The previous farmer had sold up because the farm was too small to be profitable.

Stretching away from the house, the ridged olive terraces are probably much older than the farm buildings – they may even date back to Roman or Etruscan times. The olives are part of the spirit of the house and the local traditions of the area. We decided that even if they provided only a small source of income, we would keep the history of our home alive and continue to work the farm.

The land of the sun

As far as we can tell from the records, the house has always been known as Casa del Sole. It really is 'the house of the sun'. Every morning the sun rises behind us, bathing the far valley in a lemony light. By not shining directly into the house it wakes us gently (unless Gregory or the dogs demand immediate company), and we lie in bed to watch the colour creep over the woods and hills.

In the late afternoon and evening, the sun passes over the house, setting beyond our valley. When we dine outside in summer, a glorious sunset illuminates our big stone table as we listen to the bells of the local church pealing below.

Two ridges run either side of our land, creating a basin. Tucked in this dip, the house is usually sheltered from wind and rain and we are secluded in our own small world. Our nearest neighbours sit further up the hillside, hidden in the twists of the track that link us to Pescia below. Isolated by the thickness of the trees, we've established a new method of communication with our friend Marisa on the opposite side of the valley. In late summer, usually after the crackle and clatter of an electrical storm, we signal to each other with lights, winking a greeting to confirm we still have power.

The house needs attention but the ancient landscape falling away on either side drags our eyes from the crumbling bricks and reminds us that things can't be hurried. Maybe that's why we don't feel daunted by the work ahead.

Right The farm overlooks a series of wooded valleys.
Below Steep terraces of olives fall away below the house.

Settling in

Casa del Sole welcomed us from our first night. The house had been neglected for so long that I like to think it knew we were going to bring it happiness and life, and some much needed maintenance.

On our second morning at Casa del Sole, my mother arrived, bringing Gregory.

Too tired to unpack the rest of the van, Richard at least managed to extricate and assemble our bed. This familiar piece of furniture formed a small island in the cavernous new bedroom. It felt very strange to have so much space; our old home would have fitted into a third of the farmhouse. It would now be a long walk across the kitchen from the kettle to the fridge, but I could hardly complain about that. We sank into the dents of the mattress and had our first much-needed sleep.

The next morning, Gregory arrived with his grandma. Collecting them from the airport, I noted that Gregory didn't seem to have missed us at all and was ready for the adventure of seeing our new home. He vaguely remembered the house from our first visit, or rather remembered the resident cat, who he'd already christened 'Ciao Miaow'. Delighted to be here, he played all day in the garden with the dogs and, for the first time ever, exhausted himself. We were glad to have him back with us – the team was complete.

Home finances

Despite selling our house in Yorkshire, Richard and I couldn't afford to buy Casa del Sole outright. We had saved £5,000 for essential renovations but our quotes for repairs now ran to £10,000. On top of this, we estimated that our living costs would be £12,000 a year.

The final payment for the house was due in November and we decided to apply for a 40,000 euro mortgage. I searched the internet for a suitable lender and, although living in Italy, chose an English building society for ease of communication.

The mortgage meant that we could finally complete on Casa del Sole but it also demanded regular repayments. There was no choice, the disco van would have to go back on the road. Richard decided that he'd travel back to Yorkshire a few times each month as the discos would guarantee an income of £500 a week. It was a quick fix but no long-term solution. We'd come away to spend time together as a family, not to be separated by weeks in different countries. Gregory missed his dad and we became desperate to find an Italian source of income. The house, we decided, would have to pay for itself.

Paying its way

The property comprised tumble-down farm buildings and the olive groves. We'd been told that a good harvest could bring in £3,000 – a fair sum but not enough to cover the bills. Growing additional produce would provide a degree of self-sufficiency but being subsistence farmers had not been part of the plan. We needed to find more reliable funds.

Turning half of the spacious farmhouse into self-catering holiday accommodation seemed the ideal solution. It didn't require us to speak fluent Italian, would provide instant cash and allow us to live in the other, unrenovated, half of the building. There was also the chestnut-roasting house in the grounds – we decided to restore this too and rent it out.

It didn't take long to settle in as we had little furniture apart from beds and a sofa; the vendor had left a few chairs.

The work ahead

Renovating the farmhouse to receive guests would require a lot of work. Actually 'a lot of work' is a big understatement. The house had no indoor bathroom or toilet, the water tank was made of asbestos, the wiring was ancient, the roof leaked, there was no hot water or heating and all the windows and doors needed replacing. Much of the work we just couldn't afford to start, but safe water was a priority. Prevented from working on the house until our final contract had been processed, Christian (the vendor) at least allowed us to replace the asbestos tank. We continued to wait for our final contract. And wait.

A long summer

In July all seemed set for the final signing, but Christian's *geometre* (a cross between a surveyor and a solicitor) dragged his heels and bureaucracy slowed the paperwork again. July ran into August and we were told that it would take at least another month to complete. From the celebration of Mary's Assumption on August 15th, Italy shuts down for a summer break. Even our bank stopped operating its regular hours and the shutters were sleepily drawn at unpredictable times. We hadn't anticipated this, but we weren't going to be able to change a nation's holiday habits. Unable to tackle the house, we turned our attention to the garden and waited for September.

Camping out

Living in the unrenovated farmhouse was really a form of glorified camping. The kitchen at least had an old gas cooker (good for launching an Italian cooking regime), but the bathroom situation was rather less formal.

An outdoor shower, located in a wooden shed in the garden, ran on a

The outdoor toilet comprised a seat, a bucket and a handful of sawdust; the shower was rigged in a garden shed.

rudimentary solar-powered system. On the roof, a thick coil of black hosepipe was heated by the sun; the water in the pipe was warmed and then emptied through a rusty head into the shower. That was it. On first inspection we didn't believe that such a basic system could possibly work. It soon proved to be amazingly efficient.

From mid-May to October, even when the weather was cloudy, the water was often heated to scalding temperatures. This was the start of our education in alternative forms of energy – often, the simpler the system, the more effective it was. Except in winter.

Winter in Tuscany is damp and wet. Rainy months from November to April were spent miserably poking sodden twigs into the bottom of the wood-burning stove. Temperamental and fickle, the stove would splutter expectantly then fizzle out without

producing any heat. It was now too cold to shower outside. Bathing in a tub in the lounge, our feet blistered in a measly half-inch of water, while the rest of the body shivered.

The toilet was also outdoors. Even more elementary than the shower, it comprised a bucket set in a wooden plinth and a scoop of wood shavings for a flush. I feared it would quickly attract flies and become unusable. Surprisingly it served us well, even during winter, although admittedly I wasn't the one having to empty it.

Wednesday 6th November, 6pm

It's ours! Finally, the *geometre* organised the paperwork and we completed on the house. The wait was over and Casa del Sole belonged to us. In fact the delay had been so long that we were more relieved than excited. Still, we managed to open a bottle of wine and headed to Pescia for a celebratory meal.

The kitchen is located upstairs on an open balcony (*loggia*). It will be moved indoors when renovations are complete.

Renovation

With the contract signed, we could finally start the slow process of renovating the farm. The first priority was to install some hot water and heating. The solid walls of the farmhouse meant that while the house would be lovely and cool in summer, it would never warm without heating in winter. The prospect of cold nights huddled around our wretched wood-burning stove was not appealing.

While we were waiting to sign the contract we had organised quotes for the building work and extracted promises from the builders, plumbers and electrician that they would start *subito* (straight away), as soon as the house was ours. We had also secured planning permission for the alterations we wanted to make. Planning regulations are strict in Italy, especially for old buildings. As a general rule you can make alterations inside your property but plans that affect the external walls need permission. Structures in wood (within reason) are not subject to planning permission, but anything built in stone is regulated. Creating partitions in the farmhouse for a bathroom and laundry required permission so we asked our *geometre*, Andrea, to negotiate this for us.

Andrea doesn't speak any English but he has mastered the art of speaking Italian slowly enough for us to understand. He has been absolutely key in our restoration of the house; without him we would never have found the builders, let alone been able to communicate with them. He has the expert knowledge vital for converting traditional Tuscan buildings and he is one of the few *geometres* in our area not to have been implicated in local government scandals. Of course we didn't know all this when we hired him, we were just extraordinarily lucky to find him.

Below Wooden structures, such as the new bathroom at the chestnut house, did not need planning permission.

Hot water

The plumber had promised to start work as soon as the house was ours and was as good as his word. His efficiency was no doubt encouraged by the firm influence of his wife, Guanita, who ran the office. One day in town, I visited her and explained that we were living with no hot water or heating and that I had a small child and was pregnant again. Suitably horrified, she launched an immediate rescue campaign and provided a team of plumbers as well as all the materials *pronto*.

A week later we had hot water and radiators. It was bliss. I consigned the wood-burning heater to a storage room – a monument of 'how we used to live'. Meanwhile, Gregory ran round the house, laying a hand on each radiator with a shout of 'Mummy it's HOT!'

A bathroom

The bathroom posed more of a problem. There were no facilities in the house, so we needed to adapt another room for the purpose. This meant digging out the floor of one of the downstairs *cantinas* to take pipes, building partition walls and connecting the plumbing. Richard began the arduous work of removing the floor himself while we waited for the builders to arrive. Doggedly excavating through rocks and soil for two feet, he then had to wheel the rubble to the end of our driveway where we were making a turning area for the car. It was hard physical work, but I consoled him that it would certainly shift any excess weight.

Waiting for workmen

Richard continued to dig, but there was still no sign of the builders. We

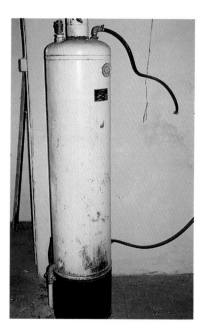

Right The old wood-burning stove was difficult to light and filled the house with smoke. Far right Our new stove.

We discovered that part of the problem was our steep dirt driveway. The building materials had already been delivered but the workmen weren't keen on carrying their tools further than a few yards. More than happy to size up the hill, the track and the mad residents, the builders would come to give a quote, would provide a start date while drawing deeply on a strong cigarette, and then never reappear. Phoning to see where they were, we would be told that they'd certainly arrive in the morning; we never discovered which morning.

Worrying that perhaps our language skills were letting us down, we enlisted Andrea's help. Somewhat comfortingly, he had the same trouble; apparently it's an Italian thing. Being a fairly rare breed and much in demand, Italian builders can pick and choose their work and won't be held to ransom by anyone – especially mad English people.

asked another firm to quote for the work and they promised to visit by the end of the week. They didn't show up either. Four more building firms were contacted; four more no-shows. We started to fear that our reputation was preceding us. The concept of going to work for 'the mad English family on the hill', who had lived all winter without a toilet or bathroom, obviously didn't appeal to the average Italian builder.

JANUARY 2003: THE BUILDERS ARE HERE

Finally, after three months, Andrea had found a building firm willing to quote and to actually turn up. I'm told we could have a bathroom in two weeks! I'm now wise to Italian timing; I don't hold my breath.

Dante, our head builder, mixes concrete for new floors in the farmhouse.

In the third week of January, the builders arrived. They heaved up our driveway in a battered truck, bringing cement mixers, tools and general disarray. We were so grateful that we immediately tried to ply them with hot drinks and biscuits. They were having none of it; they were here to work and wouldn't be delayed, even by tea.

The team was headed by Dante. Unassuming, calm and stoical, he was to become our friend and trusted advisor on all things (I nearly said to do with building, but Dante actually helped us with everything from when the shops were open to translating Gregory's Italian for us). Gregory adored him and followed him around with a trowel 'helping'.

Within a couple of days, the builders had laid a bathroom floor over Richard's excavations in the old *cantina*. Made out of concrete, it had ducts to prevent damp and reinforcements for strength. After a week we had walls to partition off two bathrooms and a laundry room, then a septic tank, then plumbing (courtesy of the plumber's wife), then plaster and then, with much excitement and ceremony – a BATHROOM SUITE.

After nine months of an outside toilet, we could finally flush. Actually, the outdoor toilet had been less frustrating than the 'bird baths' taken in the tub in the lounge or the struggle to light the wood-burning stove. Still, a functioning bathroom brought a lot of joy. I insisted on having the first go – the door closed, the light clicked on, and water, deliciously hot, gushed from the showerhead. Our outdoor facilities may have had a fantastic valley view, but this was the return of civilisation.

With extreme patience, Dante always took time to carefully explain the work in progress, despite our poor Italian. One day he and Andrea (our *geometre*) were having a heated discussion about the chestnut house. It seemed that it had no foundations and that the regular earth tremors that occur here were threatening the safety of the walls. Richard and I listened to the debate with differing degrees of comprehension. Finally, Andrea turned to us and said, in Italian, 'We're going to inject concrete under the walls and put a sliver of glass in that crack. If the glass breaks, we are in trouble as the house will fall down.' Richard nodded his head in an encouraging way and said brightly, '*Va bene*' (that's great), his standard response. The rest of us turned to him with a vehement '*Non va bene*!' and laughed – it was obvious that he hadn't grasped a word that had been said.

The farmhouse became a repository for building tools, materials and rubble as renovations continued.

Sparks fly

While the building work progressed, our electrician, Daniele, tackled the wiring. Actually, he's only a part-time electrician; his day job is in a pasta factory. The Italian electrical system is a mysterious subject and it seems that an intimate knowledge of spaghetti may indeed be the key to unravelling jumbled Tuscan electrics. Richard initially thought that he could help, but it was soon clear that wiring was best tackled by someone less likely to electrocute themself.

The electrical problems started soon after we moved in. Each time I went to make a comforting piece of toast, I got an electric shock from the toaster. Richard thought that I was just imagining it. Soon small crackles of static progressed to arm-numbing shocks. Richard still didn't believe me. One morning, a huge blast of current sent me flying across the kitchen. I was hysterical and vomiting; Richard finally had to take me more seriously. Daniele was duly summoned.

Digging around in the electrical box, Daniele found that the earth had been connected into the live wire, so that electricity was literally running through the walls of the house. I felt the shocks because I always have bare feet. Richard, lucky for him, always wears sandals. The tangled wiring was labyrinthine. The system is different to the UK – plugs don't have fuses but houses have a *salva vita* box (literally a 'life saver' box) to break the current; or rather they should have. Needless to say, there wasn't one at Casa del Sole.

Daniele came and worked as many hours as he could between pasta-making shifts. He often sent Dante into a frenzy by not turning up when needed, but he got the job done in the end. Mostly. I'm still waiting for proper plugs on the washing machine...

Below Daniele, our electrician, tackles the farmhouse wiring. **Right** The bathroom has a new floor and is ready to receive partitions and plumbing.

Learning from our experience

RENOVATING IN ITALY

Everyone fantasises about restoring a ruin into a dream house but it's good to be prepared for the pitfalls. Buying Casa del Sole was only the first hurdle; the house was in terrible condition when we arrived. We've certainly learnt that renovation is a long, hard and often expensive process.

The building

- If you are not fluent in the local language it's invaluable to enlist the help of an expert, such as an architect or *geometre*, who can speak a little English. We found Andrea, our *geometre*, simply by passing his office in Pescia. He doesn't speak much English but he is incredibly helpful and we can understand enough of his Italian to get by – not something you can take for granted.

- If you are buying any property, old or new, a thorough structural check should be undertaken by a *geometre* so you know exactly what you're letting yourself in for. At the same time, the *geometre* should check that the boundaries of the property on the title deeds match those that you are being sold, and whether there are any public rights of way or covenants on the land.

- Before buying, it is important that your *geometre* establishes whether the house is listed, if you need permission to develop the site and whether this has been granted. You need to ensure that you can actually implement any of your dream plans.

- Local geology may affect building plans, connections to water, gas and electricity supplies and also the cost of your renovations. Because of its age, our house was built without foundations, but fortunately on rock. A *geometre* should check the foundations of your house, especially if it is built on a hill – the leaning tower of Pisa leans because it was built on clay ground without foundations – it's easy to be caught out!

- Your *geometre* is NOT obliged to check whether any other developments are planned for your local area and how this might affect your property. We didn't carry out any detailed research into the immediate area around Casa del Sole because we own most of this land. Olive groves are a good indication that any building development will be limited, as olive trees are 'protected' in most areas of Italy.

- If there is even the faintest possibility that building developments may be planned around your prospective house, then ask for information from as many different local commune (government) officials as possible. Remember that it may be in their interests not to let you know.

- Consider the access route to your house if you're planning extensive renovations, as you'll need to arrange for the delivery of materials. We mistakenly assumed that goods could be delivered easily because our pathway was passable in summer. However, we took delivery of most of our materials in winter when the path was muddy and treacherous. We parted with a small fortune to hire a tractor to move supplies on to site. Even then, the builders refused to start work until it was easier for them to drive up to the house!

Utilities

- You need to establish whether the house is connected to gas, water and electricity and how these will be supplied (this is less of a concern with newer properties). At Casa del Sole we pump our water from the stream that borders our land. You need to be very careful about this type of supply as you may be taking water illegally. Your *geometre* can investigate who owns the rights and you can easily apply for these, as long as they are not owned by somebody else. It is also important to establish whether the stream dries up in summer. Ours did, so we had to apply for a 'right to draw' from another stream as well.

- It is vital to obtain a few estimates for any building work you will not undertake yourself. Andrea (our *geometre*) organised most of our quotes, although we did find our own electrician through word of mouth. Remember a quote is just that – don't expect the final bill to tally. We had occasions where the materials were much cheaper than expected but there were unforeseen problems so labour was more expensive. Always have about a 10 per cent contingency fund (or access to that amount of money) just in case.

Learning from our experience
RENOVATING IN ITALY

- If you are not connected to the main waste disposal system (many old properties are not) then you need to budget for the installation of a septic tank. Take advice from your *geometre* but don't expect this to cost any less than £5,000 (unless you can install it yourself).

- It is important to establish whether buildings are protected by any special regulations that limit extension beyond the original boundaries, internal changes and the type of building methods before you start any work. In Tuscany there are strict regulations governing building work on old properties. You can make structural alterations inside your home, but anything that affects the external walls requires permission. New structures in stone are also regulated.

- Repairing a roof is costly but essential. It's worth considering what time of year you are moving in and whether you'll have time to make any necessary repairs. Our roof desperately needs replacing but we can't afford it yet; we have had to ask the builders to patch any leaks and plan to get this work done next October.

- Replacing windows and doors may be necessary and expensive. We had great difficulty finding affordable ready-made windows and doors, or finding a carpenter to make them.

- Only attempt to do the work you know you can do properly. Richard was able to dig out foundations and undertake general carpentry. We also saved money by him labouring for the builders. Tackling the electrics, however, was another matter – in some cases it certainly pays to bring in the professionals.

- Any work on the house should be checked by your *geometre*, who has to submit a report to the commune at the end of any major renovations. Your *geometre* will advise on any work that has to be 'certified' and undertaken by a qualified professional. At Casa del Sole, the only work needing certification was the installation of a gas tank.

It is worth checking whether there is any land or any outbuildings associated with the property and whether these can be renovated or developed. Sometimes a house will have land associated with it that is not actually anywhere near the property. Building regulations are fairly strict for outbuildings, but planning permission is usually granted if you restore them in a sympathetic manner. Ordinarily, planning regulations stipulate numerous conditions, such as the installation of a bathroom or that windows cannot be altered.

Deciding the order of work is often a matter of common sense balanced with funds available. Our priority really should have been mending our roof, but we just couldn't afford this; as a consequence we'll have a lot of redecorating to do later. It's worth asking your builder for advice.

	Bradford Road YORKSHIRE	Casa del Sole TUSCANY
Market price	£105,000	£110,000
Mortgage	£35,000	40,000 euros
Number of bedrooms	3	5 (potentially 6)
Outbuildings	None	Chestnut house
Land	Small garden	15 acres
Initial renovation costs	Nil	£30,000
Future renovation costs	Nil	£30,000
Potential rental income	Nil	£7,200 per year
Potential olive oil income	Nil	£3,000 per year
Potential market value	£110,000	£300,000+
Desirability	Low	High

Windows and doors

We needed to install windows and doors in the side of the house that would be guest accommodation. Our living area would remain unmodernised until we could afford to improve it. Expert in trawling DIY superstores in the UK, we'd assumed that we could buy these items cheaply and ready made. Trooping to the local door shop in Pescia, we discovered that it would actually cost us £1,000 for seven internal doors. In Tuscany, mass production still runs a poor second to local craftsmanship. This is great news for the local economy, but it wasn't good news for us. We hadn't been able to preorder our doors and windows from a local carpenter and we had our first paying guests arriving in six weeks. Frantically we began searching for a carpenter who could at least start work on the external doors.

In the meantime, Richard decided that he would dust off his workbench and make the internal doors himself. Taking to the challenge, he knocked out a couple in record time. But the DIY road is never smooth. The next day, Dante informed him that the floor was going to be raised another two inches. The doors wouldn't fit. The workbench came out again.

We still hadn't found a carpenter to make the windows and external doors and time was running out. One day, lost (as usual) looking for the *autostrada*, we drove past a small workshop with wooden frames outside. Lurching to a halt, we went in to investigate. It was indeed a carpenter's workshop. Inside, Giuseppe screeched away with his wood saw. We explained our problem in broken Italian, hoping that our desperate arm gestures conveyed the urgency of the task. Nodding calmly, he thought he could probably finish and fit the doors and windows by our now imminent deadline. One day, I thought, our luck will run out; or maybe our winter trials without a bathroom had earned us some credit.

Below and right Giuseppe's team installed new windows. Below right Richard made the new internal doors himself.

March 2003: Progress

Giuseppe arrived with our new windows on March 31st. We had little time to spare before the arrival of our first guests, but the windows were worth the wait. Beautifully crafted, with shutters on the inside, they restored the traditional look of the house and would keep winter chills and the fierce summer sun at bay. We formed an instant working party, chipping out the rotten frames while Giuseppe and his team followed behind fitting the new ones.

We had almost finished the first stage of renovation and had more than spent our funds. All that was left was some floor cleaning and beautifying. Richard and I set about the task with force. Sometimes too much force. In one enthusiastic session, Richard managed to remove the cement between the terracotta floor tiles with a jet-wash. For his next act, he jumped off a ladder and straight through the bedroom floor into the room below. Amazingly unhurt, he picked himself up and resignedly phoned Dante. A new floor was installed. I briefly

considered renting Richard out as a circus act, but there was no time. Our first guests were due to arrive in just over one week.

The house looked different. Always beautiful, it now looked more proud of itself with lovely new windows, hanging baskets full of blooms and, inevitably, Gregory's toys scattered out the front. It had become our home and, more importantly, we felt we belonged to it. Our side of the house was unfinished, but we'd achieved all the things we'd set out to do in our first year – just!

Left The house's draughty, old windows were removed.
Below Light streams through new windows in the bedroom.

Our Land

Taking on 15 acres of woodland, olive groves, fruit trees and a vegetable plot, not to mention chickens, was a big commitment. Each season was to bring its own tasks and new surprises.

We arrived at Casa del Sole at the end of May. In Tuscany, spring is already over at this time of year and the hills are starting to warm for summer. The terraces were flooded with a patchwork of green. Bright emerald new grass contrasted with the silvery grey leaves of the olive groves and buttercups and poppies dotted the roadsides. We collected our tools and began work on the tangles of vegetation that pushed at the walls of the farmhouse.

Richard cuts wood from the land behind our house to fuel all our heating and hot water.

The valley

The landscape in this part of Tuscany falls and rises, with rolling hills dipping into low spreading plains. The hills (where we live) are scattered with farms; tiny smallholdings between the red-roofed villages that disturb the lines of olive terraces, cypress trees and woods. Down in the warmth of the plains, large farms have swept away the woods and broad squares of flowers patchwork the flat valley floors. Pescia, our local town, is Italy's largest flower exporter.

Flowers are everywhere. Farmed in the fields, wild in the roadsides and lovingly tended in gardens. At least half of the year is spent outside, so people surround themselves with roses, poppies, lavender and irises. Just about everyone with a garden also has a kitchen garden, in which they grow the widest variety of vegetables – courgettes, rocket, asparagus, aubergines, tomatoes, artichokes, beans and pumpkins – as well as herbs and fruit.

Our acres

Most houses have gardens, but Casa del Sole, with its 15 acres and 350 olive trees, is classed as a small farm. The land is divided between woodland and the olive groves. We are bounded on two sides by small streams, from which we draw our water. An old pump and a motley network of pipes link house and garden, supplying our bathroom, kitchen and Gregory's paddling pool.

At the top of our land we back on to an organic bee farm – wonderful for pollinating our olives and fruit trees. Below the house, the lower land falls away into gnarled woods full of wild boar, porcupines, foxes and pine martens. It's a secret and mysterious playground full of hidden corners; despite our best efforts and Gregory's habit of getting lost, we haven't discovered them all yet.

Similar woodlands – a mixture of pine, chestnut, oak and other deciduous trees – are found any-where on the hills that is not used for olives. Crisscrossed by hundreds of ancient pathways, you can tramp freely along miles of dusty woodland track looking for shade or nuts. The land is all privately owned but Italy's 'right to roam' policy means that you won't be trespassing. Cutting down trees is less easy. A special police force, the *forestale*, patrols the woods to protect them from fire and illegal logging and a special licence is needed if you want to cut down large trees such as chestnut and pine.

Woodland must be managed with dead branches removed, dangerous trees felled and new ones planted. Dense and overgrown, the woodland at Casa del Sole had obviously been neglected for some time. Repairing the house was our first priority, but we applied for a state grant to help us coax the trees into some kind of order. We'll start work in the woods when this finally comes through.

Dense woodland of chestnut, oak, birch and pine trees covers any parts of the hills not terraced for olive groves.

Resources

As we have a large and renewable source of wood, we decided to run all our winter heating and hot water from a wood-burning stove. Most old houses in the area use this form of heating and Casa del Sole already had a tall, cylindrical old stove in the lounge. Using wood for fuel is only economic if you have your own supply; for us it is very efficient. My only worry is that Richard won't return in one piece when he goes to chop trees – he's more than a little accident prone.

Chestnut time

The woods are full of chestnut trees that produce nuts in late autumn. A traditional source of food in Tuscany, the nuts were gathered and roasted in the little chestnut house in our grounds. Spread out on the floor upstairs, a fire would be lit below until they'd turned toasty brown.

Each year nuts are still collected and eaten whole or ground to make chestnut flour, a substitute for wheat which doesn't thrive in this area. Pescia celebrates the annual harvest with chestnut flour pancakes, stuffed with ricotta cheese and Nutella (made locally). Warm buttery currents drift over the market square in November, as vendors stoke braziers for the fiesta. Our friends Sonia and Luca prepared pancakes for us as chestnut-gathering reached its peak. Anticipating rich, sticky delights we chewed stolidly through the grey woody rounds. Perhaps an acquired taste. We decided that our chestnut house would be better used housing guests than chestnuts.

The wild boar that roam the woods are more dedicated chestnut fans. In season, the nuts are their favourite food; out of season, my plants top the list. Our dogs' main task is chasing the greedy hogs from my vegetable patch when they come on their regular raids. Naturally shy, the boars can be ferocious when challenged. I secretly thank the dogs for scaring them off as I walk up the steep path to our house in the dark.

The thriving boar suggest that the woodland is an ideal home for pigs. I'd planned to purchase some piglets this spring, but decided that a new baby and new piglets might be too much to manage. Next year I'll not be put off and the boar will have to fight it out with my piggies for their share of the chestnuts.

Chestnut trees in the woods produce nuts in late autumn which are roasted and eaten whole or ground up for flour.

Our Land

A KITCHEN GARDEN

There was no garden at Casa del Sole when we arrived, but I'd picked the perfect spot on our first viewing. I'd transform the thatch of weeds between the house and the olive groves into my vegetable patch.

A jungle of rampant grass and wild mint covered a flat shelf of land between the house and the olive terraces below. Near to a tumble-down greenhouse and our water supply, this seemed the perfect spot for a vegetable patch. Starting from scratch meant I could plan the garden just as I wanted it. The only downside was that new beds would mean lots of digging – not my favourite job in 40-degree heat.

We weren't permitted to work on the house while we waited to sign our final contract, so we spent the

summer months tackling the garden. The first task was to clear the weeds and grass, then mark out the new beds using twigs and twine. Next the digging. Three days of back-straining work, although Gregory did his best with a bucket and small spade.

Christian, the previous owner, alerted me to a family of cheeky porcupines that live in the woods. Nightly poachers, they like nothing better than troughing home-grown vegetables so a new fence was a priority. Leaning on our new three-foot netting, Christian laughed at our effort, 'Don't you know porcupines jump?' I was dubious but not having seen an Italian porcupine, anything was possible. Gregory was less easily led and rumbled the joke, 'Porkie Pines don't jump mummy!' He was right.

Above Clearing the garden was our main task over the summer. Left New seedlings start off the vegetable patch.

To market

Seeds must be started in February and sown at the beginning of March. It was June by the time I was ready to plant, so I decided to buy seedlings instead and visited the local market. I actually had no idea what I should plant and when, but assumed that they'd only be selling seasonal items. Speaking no Italian but clutching a phrase book, the frenetic Saturday morning market was more than a little daunting.

Weaving through the stalls, I spied a market garden supplier and scanned the seedlings on offer. Some I recognised, but most I could identify only as something green and leafy. Relying on my favourite saying, 'shy bairns get nowt', I decided to give the seasoned stallholder the benefit of my full Italian vocabulary. I launched into '*mi dispiace, sono inglese, non parlo italiano*' (I'm sorry, I'm English and don't speak Italian), while gesticulating wildly in the direction of some seedlings. Without pause, he rattled off a monologue (probably essential advice on how to keep slugs from your courgettes)

which I'd no hope of following. I'd understandably confused him by being telling him, in perfect Italian, that I couldn't speak the language.

The incident ended with lots of laughter (and embarrassment on my part) and much pointing at plants saying '*si*' (yes). Everyone was pleasantly amused by my awful attempts and so helpful that I returned home with most of what I needed, a lot of what I wanted and even more of what I didn't want. I realised that the only answer was to visit the market with fistfuls of cash to pay for my mistakes.

Left The bustling market is always full of free advice.
Below Too late to plant seeds, the market provided seedlings.

Planting out

Armed with a couple of trusted gardening manuals (albeit for English soil and climate), I began to plant. In my garden in Yorkshire I'd toiled away trying to grow all sorts of vegetables and herbs with little success. The heavy clay soil meant that the only things to prosper were onions, potatoes and strawberries. Here in Italy it was a different story. The soil is light and easy to manage and the strong sun entices the plants out of the ground. The problems are almost the reverse: you have to water frequently, be careful to limit unnecessary growth and keep weeds in their place (on the compost heap).

I planted beans, carrots, onions, peppers, beetroot, potatoes, leeks, pumpkins, cucumbers, courgettes, melons, aubergines, strawberries and of course, lovely Italian tomatoes. I couldn't wait to see how they'd grow.

There were certainly some mistakes. I planted the onions and carrots at the wrong time. My melons were stunted by an unidentifiable disease and my potatoes were munched by a plague of Colorado beetles. But the successes certainly made up for the disasters. My first home-grown cucumber was possibly my biggest achievement and Gregory can't wait for summer to come around again as these are his favourite.

The less predictable disasters were actually manmade. One afternoon Richard decided to 'help out' by strimming some weeds – in fact my strawberry patch and new rhubarb plants. He and Gregory are now banished from the garden unless accompanied by a *responsible* adult.

Our fruits

There was no vegetable patch when we moved to the farm, but the garden soon revealed a number of fruit trees. At the top of the olive groves, a small, rounded tree bore a crop of downy golden apricots in June. July brought peaches, cherries, redcurrants and white currants.

The light soil and strong sun helped to produce a good first crop of vegetables and fruits in the garden at Casa del Sole.

Beautiful tart jewels on bushes behind the farmhouse. In August the orchard fruits ripened and we had pears, apples and persimmons. To the left of the house, a small terrace of gnarled and twisted vines bore a crop of black grapes at the end of August. Finally in November, clusters of whiskery kiwi fruit emerged between the leaves of another set of vines, found twisting behind the house. I rushed to get a good gardening book for advice on care and pruning. I'm still not sure I've mastered the pruning of the kiwis, but we'll find out this autumn.

By midsummer there was such a glut of fruit that we were having difficulty collecting it all, let alone eating it. The weather is so hot at this time of year that picked fruit doesn't even last through the night without starting to ferment. I made huge vats of jam and chutney. I dried fruit; I froze fruit; I made fruit sorbets, puddings and compotes. We ate as much fresh fruit as was humanly possible (given our toilet facilities); even the chickens ate fruit. In the end, much of the harvest was wasted. We just couldn't process it quickly enough. This year we'll be better prepared. We've already started collecting bottles and jars, we've bought a bigger freezer and my jam recipes are at the ready.

Cider

One of the largest bounties last year was our apple crop. Just as I realised that we had enough apples to feed a small town on a very hungry day, the overnight fermentation of our fruit

gave me an idea. Cider. It was my birthday in early August and I asked Richard if he'd buy me a fruit press so we could make cider and later our own wine. He didn't need much persuading so we visited the agricultural supplies shop in Lucca and bought the largest press they had.

Friends over from England helped pick the apples and Richard and I started on the pressing. It was hot work forcing the apples through the press and the sweet juices attracted the flies. We were covered in a film of stickiness and I had difficulty stopping Gregory drinking all the juice as it squelched from the press.

After pressing, we decanted the juice into demijohns and fermentation began. Six months later we were ready to sample our Tuscan scrumpy. It was delicious. A lovely cloudy golden yellow, tangy and appley fresh. We braved the giggles of our Italian neighbours who thought we were mad trying to make 'wine' out of our apples. Invited round for a tasting, they told us that they usually let their apple surplus rot. I think we had the better plan.

With more apples than we could possibly eat, we decided to buy a fruit press and try making our own cider.

Learning from our experience

MANAGING THE LAND

The land at Casa del Sole – 15 acres of woodland and olive groves – is as important as the house. Its management is a full-time job, but it has given us new challenges, a source of income and a new self-sufficient lifestyle.

Your land

■ When buying a property, consider how much land you actually need and what you're going to do with it – sometimes less is best. Caring for 15 acres is a full-time job, certainly not a low-maintenance garden for weekend relaxation.

■ If you are buying a working farm you are entitled to a discounted rate of purchase tax. The farm may also qualify for status as an *agriturismo* – a working farm that takes in paying guests. This entitles you to discounted purchase tax, income tax relief, grants for renovation from the EU and Italian government and subsidies on farm machinery. It is worthwhile employing an agronomer, who will organise everything from IVA (VAT) registration to subsidies or registration as an organic producer.

■ You are legally required to maintain your property at a safe level (to avoid the risk of fire) in rural Italy. This means you must have the time, skills and physical fitness to manage your land, or enough money to pay someone to help. We had some experience of growing produce and keeping animals, but managing the olives and the woodland are skilled jobs and it's been a steep learning curve.

■ Double-check your boundaries. We were very woolly about where our land started and finished and mistakenly cut down a neighbour's trees, thinking they were ours.

■ The 'right to roam' policy gives public access to your land. To erect any fence, you must apply to the local government commune for permission and have a good reason (such as keeping livestock secure).

Planting out

- If you are planning extensive reorganisation of your land, including clearance and replanting, check local regulations. Tuscan olive trees, for instance, are protected by law and cannot be cut down. Likewise, large chestnut or pine trees on or near your property may be protected.

- Local conditions will affect any plans for your land. Soil, climate and the seasons are all different to the UK and even vary locally.

- With more sun in summer and plenty of rain in winter plants (and weeds) thrive. Even a small vegetable patch involves lots of hard work.

- Seeds or plants bought from England will probably not thrive in Italy. Most UK seeds are bred for a much cooler climate and often won't even germinate in the Italian summer heat. Having said this, I brought my prized strawberry plants from England (unaware that this was illegal) and they have flourished, providing a double crop last year.

- Planting times will differ to those in English gardening books because of seasonal difference and local preference. Italians plant according to a traditional 'lunar calendar', which is available at most garden centres. This gives advice on what to plant and when. I now have enough Italian to decipher this, but I'm sure I'll still make some planting mistakes.

- Rotation is the secret to a healthy garden and good crops. As a general rule, never plant the same crop in an area twice and rotate root vegetables with leaf.

- Have the right tools for the job. Making do with the wrong equipment wastes precious time and energy. I have yet to take my own advice on this and still struggle with a decrepit old garden fork whose handle regularly falls off – maybe Richard will treat me to a new one for my birthday.

- If you are in any doubt about what to plant, take a sneaky look at what other people are growing in their gardens. I am regularly caught peering over walls and fences eyeing up other people's vegetable patches.

- Good planning pays off. When planning your garden consider the essential elements of sun, shade, soil and particularly easy access to water. In Italy, water is a prized commodity in summer and diverting drainpipes or saving washing water may be the only way to maintain a regular supply for your plants.

Learning from our experience

KEEPING ANIMALS

Part of our dream in taking on a farm was to keep whatever animals we wanted. So far our livestock includes only chickens, cats and dogs; next year pigs and sheep are planned. All require daily attention.

- If you've no experience of keeping livestock, start small. Begin with a few chickens and work upwards. Animal husbandry takes skill and time.

- Keeping animals is a big commitment. If you go away, even for one night, you will need to have someone on hand to check on your stock, shut them in and feed and water them.

- Animals need shelter from the rain, and particularly from the sun during summer. Pets from the UK may take time to adjust to new conditions and can suffer in extremes of temperature.

- Adequate, clean water is essential. You will need to ensure that there is a good water supply near any animal enclosures.

- Take precautions to keep pets and livestock safe from wild predators. Foxes may take chickens and cats. One of our dogs received a nasty gash from a wild boar.

- Protect your garden from your own (and wild) animals with an adequate fence. Chickens, for example, love scratching up seedlings. Last year our chickens discovered that they loved cabbages and I lost a whole crop.

- Some animals don't mix. Turkeys, for example, should not be kept with hens as they harbour a disease fatal to chickens. Ask advice or consult a good reference book before buying any animals.

- If you are buying livestock to eat, don't give them names and always regard them as dinner. We didn't follow this advice and consequently can't contemplate eating any of our chickens. I'm hoping my love of bacon will override my fondness for the pigs next year.

Animals

One of our dreams was to have enough land to keep whatever animals took our fancy. The 15 acres at Casa del Sole meant this was finally a possibility.

My parents had always kept chickens, ducks and goats, and even a sheep at one time, so animal husbandry was no mystery to me. Richard, however, knew very little; I even had to explain the chicken and egg process before we got started.

Despite our plans for flocks and herds, we've actually found that our domestic dogs from the UK are the most valued animals on the farm. We are surrounded by woods which are home to all manner of wild creatures. The dogs keep a busy night-time patrol, fending off wild boar and porcupines which come to steal vegetables from the garden, badgers which steal chickens and foxes which take anything smaller than themselves, including cats.

The first, and so far only, new livestock we've introduced are the chickens. There was already a rickety chicken house at Casa del Sole, so Richard restored it and we bought ten young hens. These included Henny, Penny, Gladys and Gregory's favourite, Daphne. Within two weeks they were laying an average of six eggs a day. By autumn, they had become so prolific that I considered asking the builders if we could pay them in eggs.

Since then, we've lost three of the chickens. One insisted on sleeping outside and was taken by a fox; another was bitten by one of our dogs, who had problems telling the difference between wild animals and our own; and most recently, Daphne passed away after suffering a stroke. We have, however, gained a cockerel from our friend Marisa. He's been christened Henry and struts around thinking himself very lucky to have seven ladies to look after. Next year we're hoping to keep him on his toes with pigs and perhaps even sheep.

Our dog, Brook, minds the chickens. The dogs have been invaluable for keeping wild animals out of the garden.

THE OLIVES

If the garden is my domain then the olive groves belong to Richard.
The olives are a valuable cash crop but more than that, they are a way
of life in Tuscany, lying at the heart of the culture of the region.

The olives

It's thought that olives have been grown in Tuscany since Etruscan times. The steep hillsides provide perfect drainage for the trees, which don't like to have wet roots. Even if they have no terraces, most people in our area keep at least one olive tree in a pot. We've got 350 trees.

When we took over Casa del Sole we knew nothing about olive farming. We did know, however, that caring for the groves was an essential part of our new life. You can taste the land in the oil and

we're linked to our neighbours by the traditions surrounding the growing, picking and processing of the fruit. Olives rule the local community.

Tuscan olives are reputed to produce the highest quality oil in Italy. A lovely golden green, it has a distinctive fruity flavour that changes according to the type of olive and how they're picked and processed. If you pick early, the taste is spicy and rich as the olives yield a small amount of strong-flavoured oil. If the olives ripen for longer, they give more, but lower quality oil with a higher acidity level. We could only hope that our olives produced good oil and that we managed to harvest and press them successfully. We were relying on money from the olive harvest to pay the bills.

People in the area also cure olives for eating. It's a long process involving repeatedly washing and soaking the olives in brine. The method was in fact so long-winded that I forgot about my jars and the olives festered in the cupboard. I hoped our attempts to produce oil were going to be more successful.

Reviving the farm

From May to November the olives needed little attention. The groves were the only part of the property that had not been neglected. The previous owner had relied on income from the oil to pay his bills so the trees had been loved and carefully tended. He had pruned, tidied and harvested on his own, an amazing feat for just one man.

The general upkeep of the olives is simple but time consuming. Christian, the former owner, had given us a few pointers but Luciano became our guru. Luciano is one of our closest neighbours, living just on the other side of the valley. He's been producing olive oil for over 30 years and he knows what he's doing. It's delicious. We phone him for advice each time there's something we don't understand and he does his best to explain in terms suited to our still rudimentary Italian. We couldn't run the farm without him.

Maintaining the groves

Our first important task in the groves was grass-cutting. During summer the grass between the trees must be kept low to the ground to prevent fire. This sounds easy, but there are seven acres to cut regularly, the terraces are narrow and the terrain steep. We began strimming the grass, as Christian had advised, but with vegetation still waving around our knees after hours in the groves, we realised we were getting no-where fast. Richard, feeling decisive, stormed to town and ordered a top-of-the-range lawnmower. Still hard work on a hot day, we could at least trundle more quickly through the groves, leaving ridges of cut grass in our wake.

The grassy banks of the terraces must also be cut. Unlike the mowing, this is my favourite job. Early in the morning, while the air is light and cool, Richard and I strim the grass from the banks while Gregory sleeps. Next year, I'm going to introduce some sheep to see if these organic mowing machines can help us keep our grass in order.

Below and right In summer strimming and mowing the grass in the olive groves is essential to minimise fire risk.

Harvest

During the summer the olives had slowly ripened from tiny buds to glossy green and black fruits. By the beginning of November it was finally time to begin the harvest. We knew it must be time to pick as the local town hummed with talk of little else. Queuing for groceries at the supermarket people would anxiously ask each other, 'Have you started picking yet?' 'No, no, I'm waiting for the wind to turn', or 'Yes, we've already taken our first to the mill'. Olives are still picked by hand on most farms to prevent bruising

(bruised olives ferment and produce a lower quality oil), so it's a very labour-intensive process. It took us two months to finish.

Large nets are spread like giant picnic rugs under the trees to collect the fruit as they fall. Our nets had come with the house, but we soon discovered that we didn't have nearly enough. As one tree was stripped, the nets would have to be moved to the next. Many an argument ensued about whose turn it was to move them; next year we'll be investing in a few more nets.

Once the nets are in place, you reach up into the tree and drag your hands down the twiggy branches, stripping the olives away. As with most traditional methods, this is an acquired knack and good balance certainly helps when climbing the trees for fruits tucked in the upper branches. Fortunately, no one fell out of their tree this season but Richard still had calloused fingers four months after the harvest from all the picking.

At the end of each day we collected our olives into a large trough and removed the stalks and leaves by hand. A time-consuming, laborious process, we tried to make it more fun by combining it with a beer and a chat about what had happened in the day, who had moved most nets and who was the best olive cleaner. It was such a simple task that Gregory could also join in and feel like he was really part of farm life. The olives then had to be spread on a floor for at least three days (but no longer than nine days) to allow them to dry slightly. It is vital that they are kept free from frost or damp and we thought hard about the perfect location. Gregory's bedroom provided the answer. Temporarily ousted from his bed by the harvest, he was forced to take refuge in our bedroom while the olives dried.

Left Large nets are spread under the olive trees to catch the fruit as they are stripped from the branches by hand.

Pressing

The local mill is in the neighbouring village, Borgo a Buggiano. While the town retains its cobbled streets and crumbling plaster charm, the mill is a futuristic industrial unit on the outskirts. Almost all of the old Tuscan olive mills have closed, but most businesses are still small private *frantoios* (mills) rather than large factories. Despite the modernity of the buildings, the actual cold-pressing process also remains the same – the olives are just processed by high-tech machine rather than by hand and water power.

With our first pressing appointment made, we loaded the van and drove the olives down to the mill. The procedure at the mill is carefully regimented. A technician weighs the olives, you are given a receipt, and take your place in the queue. No one took their eyes off their olives during processing in case they were accidentally pressed in with some-one else's crop (a veritable disaster for both parties).

A few seasoned olive experts wandered over to inspect our fruits.

Above After picking, stalks and leaves were removed from the olives. *Above right* Two stone wheels crush the olives to a paste at the start of pressing.

To the mill

To secure your own pressing at the mill you need a minimum weight of 250 kilos of olives. Without this, our olives might have been processed communally and we would have only received a percentage of the oil. We were determined to have our first bottle of vintage Casa del Sole oil; nothing else would have tasted as good. By November 6th we had enough olives to make a trip to the mill. We had booked our pressing slots in October, a month before the harvest, and had guessed that we would probably need one pressing every week, weather permitting. This actually worked out quite well and we only had to cancel a couple of visits due to rain.

They were hardy looking *contadini* (country folk) and we were gratified at their satisfied grunts of approval.

The olives were washed and the remaining leaves and twiggy bits removed. Then into the mashing pit, where the stones were removed and two enormous wheels ground the olives to a thick paste – the first part of the actual pressing.

The whole process took about two hours. Suddenly a lovely rich green stream ran from the other end of the machine – our *prima spremitura* (first pressing). Traditionally olive oil was stored in large terracotta urns, but like everyone else we collected our pressing in rather unromantic plastic cans, taking it home to the 100 litre storage tanks installed in one of the *cantinas*.

Part of the procedure of pressing your olives is to hang around and chat with other growers at the mill. By November our Italian was improving so we passed the time with all manner of neighbours from large producers to people who just tended a few trees in their garden. The olive mill was like a private members club – the more olives you harvested and the more times you visited the mill, the more you were accepted. On our six visits we often saw the same faces and would end up earnestly discussing the year's crop, acidity levels and the poor picking weather – general opinion was that it had rained far too much that season. By the end of the harvest we had made some firm friends and were even arriving to loud hails of '*Ciao, l'inglese!*' (Hello the English).

Celebration

It is traditional for both the grower and processor to celebrate the first pressing of your olive harvest with a feast. On our first visit to the mill, we had seen a vast room filled with trestle tables and an open oven. On our second visit the tables were laid and women in headscarves and pinnies scurried from one to the other with mountains of food. A wrinkled old man stoked the indoor barbecue while a noisy crowd, who obviously all knew each other, arrived calling greetings. We thought that it must be some sort of fiesta or even a wedding. Finally grandfather trotted into the room triumphantly bearing a large bottle of translucent new oil. Everyone cheered loudly, clapped and kissed each other. Caught up in warmth of the occasion, it really was inspiring and touching to see a whole family (at least 30 of them) celebrating the culmination of a year's hard graft. We promised ourselves that we would hold a party like this next harvest.

Olive growing, picking and processing ties the local community together

The oil: green gold

For oil to be 'extra virgin' it must have an acidity level of less than one per cent. For it to be 'Tuscan extra virgin' it must have levels of less than 0.6 per cent. Our oil had an average acidity of 0.4 per cent. It was top quality. Bruising the olives when picking, using too much heat when processing, and a small olive-burrowing mosquito can all increase acidity. We had blundered through our first harvest but we had miraculously produced premium-grade organic oil. We kept about 70 litres for ourselves and sold the rest to family and friends. Olive oil was no longer an expensive luxury – I even started using it to fry chips – the sacrilege!

Our only mistake with the harvest was storage-related. We knew that the oil should be stored in a cool place, but didn't realise that as it was organic (with no additives) it would start to solidify below 4ºC. One evening in mid-January I went to collect some oil from the storage tank. Removing the metal lid, all our gorgeous oil appeared to have turned into a thick, sludgy soap. I was on the phone to Luciano (our trusted friend and olive guru) straight away. He calmly assured me that this was really quite normal and that when the weather warmed up, the oil would turn liquid again. He was right, but it did mean that we spent winter scooping oil out of the tanks with a tablespoon and defrosting it in a dish on the stove. Bottling some oil in advance and keeping it in a warmer store room would have been a far easier solution.

Pruning

The olive year ends with pruning. This is the most difficult task connected with the olives and must be completed after the harvest but before April. We were told that it takes a lifetime to learn, and then you die (I think this might be a Tuscan joke). Everyone we have met has a different method and each region in

Italy has different traditions. The only certainty is that no one agrees on the method for pruning olives.

As most olives are hand-picked it's important that the trees don't get too tall and that they are pruned regularly to keep up yields. In Tuscany, trees are pruned on a three-year cycle. In the first year, the tree must be pruned hard and produces little fruit. In the second year, the tree is pruned to shape (a goblet shape with an open middle to allow lots of sunshine to reach the budding olives), but not too heavily, and the yield is better. Finally in the third year, the tree is pruned lightly and (hopefully) a bumper crop of olives is delivered. Ideally your grove should be divided into three sections so that you can stagger the pruning and maintain your oil production at a regular level.

Learning about the techniques involved translating the advice of our well-meaning neighbours from Italian to English, then sifting through the various theories to find a likely system. The good news was that we were told that you can't actually kill an olive tree unless you freeze it for a long time – even Richard can't manage to do this by mistake.

Still busy with house renovations and looking after our first guests we haven't tackled the pruning yet. We have, however, booked a lesson with Luciano who has promised to come over and show us the basics. This will leave Richard with only three weeks to prune 350 trees. Some of them might have to be on a longer pruning rotation than others…

Above Richard hand-picks our olives during harvesting.
Left Our neighbour Luciano is renowned for his olive oil.

Learning from our experience

THE OLIVES

Olive farming is steeped in traditional skills and knowledge. We're still beginners, but our first harvest has taught us something of how to care for the trees, process the olives and enjoy the proceeds – lovely oil.

- For olive oil to be 'extra virgin' it must contain less than 1% oleic acid. High acid levels give a harsher flavour and lower quality oil. Our oil had an acid level of 0.4% – it was excellent quality.

- There are no short cuts to producing good oil. Harvesting at the wrong time, bruising the olives or exposing them to heat during processing can all increase acidity. Despite the hard work, it was certainly worthwhile picking by hand and taking care that the olives were properly dried, cold pressed and stored.

- Strong-tasting Tuscan oil is best used as a condiment – locals sprinkle it on salads, dip bread into it, make *bruschetta* (toasted bread drizzled with oil and rubbed with garlic). I use it for everything, even frying chips.

- Traditional farming methods are organic – no artificial fertilisers and pesticides are used. This guarantees the good flavour of the olives, but means that all olive tree cuttings must be gathered and burned immediately to prevent infestation by pests and diseases.

- Olive oil keeps for up to two years and needs to be stored in a cool (but not cold) dark place. Pure oil solidifies at about 4°C (although it will 'thaw out' when warmed).

- Timing is a crucial factor when picking olives as ripeness determines quality and taste. Tuscan oil is usually strong-tasting and fruity because the olives are picked quite young (when their acid levels are low).

- Flavoured oils are easy to make. My favourites are chilli oil, a lemon oil – great on fish – and oil with garden herbs. Great for gifts (or yourself).

Olio alle erbe aromatiche
Aromatic herb oil

Tarragon, rosemary or thyme can all be used to make delicious oil for drizzling on salads or for rubbing into meat before roasting, grilling or barbecuing.

120 g fresh herbs
480 ml extra virgin olive oil

Wash and dry the herbs, removing any woody stems.

Place the herbs in a sterilised bottle (see Hints & Tips, page 159). Using a funnel, add the oil and seal. Store in a cupboard or cool, dark place for about two weeks.

Strain the oil, discarding the leaves.

Pour the oil into a clean, sterilised bottle.

Olio dei peperoncini rossi
Red chilli oil

Bottles of this spicy oil are always passed around in local restaurants for pouring over crusty bread or onto pizza or pasta. I've managed to grow a few chilli plants in the garden so now I make my own.

6 small red chillies
480 ml extra virgin olive oil

Wash and dry the chillies. Place them in a sterilised bottle (see Hints & Tips, page 159). Using a funnel, pour the oil into the bottle.

Seal the bottle and store in a cupboard or cool, dark place. The oil will keep well for up to one year.

The spiciness of the oil will depend on the heat and number of the chillies as well as the age of the oil.

Add fewer chillies if you want a milder oil; more if you prefer a hotter taste.

Olio al limone
Lemon oil

This oil makes a lovely marinade for fish or chicken, or can just be brushed on just before grilling. The fresh citrussy flavour is an instant reminder of summer.

2 lemons
salt
480 ml extra virgin olive oil

Wash and dry the lemons then slice them very thinly.

Place the lemon slices in a dish and sprinkle with salt. Leave for about 30 minutes.

Transfer the lemons to a large sterilised jar (see Hints & Tips, page 159), add the oil and seal. Leave for one month in a cupboard or cool, dark place.

Strain the oil into sterilised bottles.

Day to Day

Moving country means adjusting to a different way of life as well as new surroundings. Getting to grips with new ways of working, school and health-care systems is all part of the process.

In England, Richard and I worked incredibly hard so we could go on holiday to escape. In Italy we work even harder, but while we work we feel like we're on holiday. Harvesting the olives, caring for guests or repairing the house improves our life in real terms not just financially.

Daily living also means trying to be responsible contributors to our new community. We buy locally; we barter goods with other producers; we share machinery with neighbours. In the UK this type of lifestyle has all but disappeared, but here in Tuscany it's quite normal.

Nine-to-five

In the UK, we worshipped the clock and daily life ran to a sergeant-major schedule. Time to get up, work, care for Gregory, eat, sleep, gym (on a good day). Now, I only wear my watch so I remember to collect Gregory from school. Very few things have deadlines – the olive trees won't wither if we don't prune them today; the house won't collapse if a wall isn't built this week; we won't starve if we don't have dinner until 10pm (although if we don't have any dinner there might be a few complaints). We are as free as it is possible to be while still completing work on the farm.

The flip-side is that this requires motivation. It's easy to become demoralised when things go wrong or to become lazy and complacent because there's no sense of urgency. Being half of a couple has been part of the solution. Running our own businesses before the move also helped. We tend to motivate each other and know when a bit of extra encouragement is needed. Last summer I was so demoralised by the debilitating heat that I took to my

bed for most of the day. Richard allowed me to indulge myself for a short while but after a few days he told me in no uncertain terms to pull my socks up and get some work done. Needless to say, I didn't like it at the time, but he was right.

Nature's rhythm

The year's seasons rather than work meetings now dictate our daily schedule. Surprisingly, this has even changed our sleep patterns. When Richard was running discos in the UK he arrived home late, while I went to bed early and rose early. We were always disturbing each other and dreaded the alarm clock. Now, since our only worry is getting Gregory to school on time, the alarm has been replaced by the deafening calls of chaffinches on the roof. Obviously this means that in winter we sleep later and in summer we get up early.

The new pattern is intrinsic to our new lifestyle. In summer we need to finish any hard physical work before it gets too hot (around 11am), so we work from 7 to 11am and then rest. We have a sleep, I cook, we go for a swim at our local pool. When the heat finally drains out of the hills around 6pm, we return to pottering in the garden, tending to the guests or organising the house. It means that we have more time together during the day. In winter, we wake later, take Gregory to school and then work through the day to make use of the light. Daily life runs to the rhythm of the year and our body clocks, not to an artificial time scale; we certainly feel healthier for it.

Right Office work dictated our daily schedule in the UK.
Far right The school run is now our only fixed appointment.

Working life in Italy involves spending more time together as a family, whether doing tasks on the farm or at play.

Work ethic

I have fallen in love with the Italian work ethic – the more successful you are, the less you have to work. In the UK if you run your own company, do well and are in demand, you work all the hours you can. Time spent at the office seems to have become a competitive status symbol. In Italy, having a balanced life is the primary objective. This means that when you've established yourself and command sufficient wages to pay the bills, you try to limit your hours and expand your free time. Even my highly qualified and busy doctor only works a six-hour day so she can spend quality time with her family. There's no denying that money is essential and family life can be constraining, but no one seems to have lost sight of the fact that wealth can make you comfortable but can't buy you happiness. I hope this won't change and am relying on the fact that Italians can be impressively stubborn and usually ignore the bad practices of other cultures.

Business as usual

One of the best quirks that I've come across in Tuscan work life is the phenomenon of Monday morning closing. When we first arrived we were confused to find many shops with their shutters pressed shut, a layer of dust still settled from the weekend. 'Why,' we asked, 'would shops not open at the start of the working week?' The obvious answer was, 'If you dread Monday mornings, the best way to deal with them is not to have them.' Quite right too.

Many businesses can shut when they want because they are family run. It is perfectly acceptable to put a sign on your door saying *chiuso per ferie* (closed for holidays). In fact, most of Italy shuts down in August. The 15th of the month is Assumption Day, a key point in the Catholic year. Of course it's a public holiday (there are no shortage of these), but I suspect the main reason for the mass closure of industry, shops and banks for at least a week is that it's just too hot to work. As the sun pounds the yellowing hills everyone craves the beach and heads for sand and cool water. Last year in August our wood-merchant, Carlo, went to Viareggio for two weeks, as did many of our other friends. Viareggio is the nearest beach, just 40 minutes by car, but there is no desire to explore further afield – as with the food, why go elsewhere when it's so good here? There's no pressure to fly to Thailand, to visit Disneyworld, to see the sights; escaping home and work for quality family time is enough.

Numerous public holidays and practices such as Monday closing affect business hours and working life in Italy.

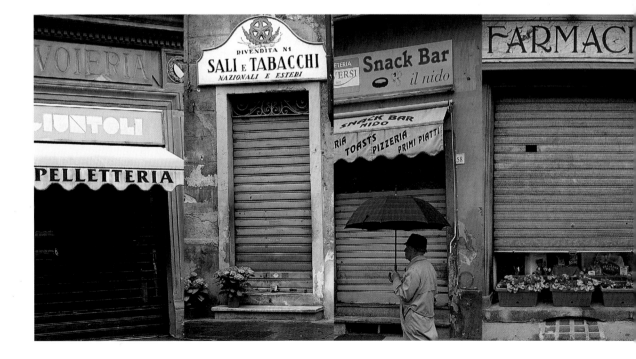

To work

Tuscan life has dissolved our divisions between home, family time and work. In the process, we've unintentionally reverted to a more archaic version of the family. Richard carries out the building, heavy farming and other manual work, while I tend the kitchen garden, organise the guest accommodation and do most of the cooking. It is simply a matter of practicalities – I haven't got the strength and certain technical skills that Richard has developed and he can't cook or raise vegetables, yet. We share the responsibility for Gregory jointly and finances are generally ignored by both of us. We are all happy with this situation. It means that we get to work together as a family but have our own jobs and avoid driving each other completely nuts.

A more equal share of the child-care has been another advantage of the move. In Yorkshire, working from home was convenient because it provided cheap office space and I could (in theory) watch Gregory and work at the same time. But work and home life pulled in opposite directions and both suffered. Tuscan living is more flexible – Richard and I can both work and both look after Gregory. We fit our chores around Gregory's needs and with many of them, such as gardening, olive picking and looking after the animals, he can actually join in. This makes care during school holidays less of a concern and negates the concept of maternity leave. Italians are entitled to five months' maternity leave on 80 per cent pay. Our more self-sufficient lifestyle offers a less rigid structure. Now expecting our second baby and, ever the optimist, I'm hoping to resume my daily routine soon after the birth. This wouldn't have been possible in the UK unless I'd either paid for childcare or we survived on Richard's wages alone.

For Richard, work now means early mornings in the farm workshop instead of late nights behind the disco decks.

Money matters

When we first moved to Casa del Sole, Richard returned to the UK for four days each week to run the disco business that funded our mortgage and renovations. He commuted for eight stressful and energy-sapping months, continuing with the house repairs on the days he was in Italy. By February we'd finally completed the guest accommodation and taken enough bookings to risk a drop in income. He handed over the business to one of his employees and we were free to dedicate our energies to the house and to each other.

If Richard hadn't been able to continue his UK work for any reason, our financial contingency plan was that I'd teach English and he would labour for a local builder. We would have done anything to stay, so we tried to explore all our options.

In Tuscany we enjoy a better quality of life, but we certainly don't have as much disposable income as we had in the UK. A decision to re-evaluate our priorities was part of the move, and new cars and expensive holidays now come far down the list.

Living in a rural community we've also found that currency doesn't always mean money – bartering is a common method of exchange. Our chickens produce more eggs than we use, so I swap half a dozen for a loaf of bread made by Marisa's husband, Rudolfo. Luciano has too many lettuces so he swaps them for a few aubergines. The trick is to have items that other people want. At the moment we only have the eggs – the jams and chutneys I made last year kept us through the winter and provided gifts for friends but there was no surplus to sell or barter. We have less money than ever and a more erratic income, but it's clear we're not going to starve.

Gardening, harvesting and preserving our produce, as well as caring for the chickens, are now important daily work.

Day to Day

HOLIDAY GUESTS

Running our holiday accommodation is now an essential part of our work in Tuscany. The business pays for the bulk of our mortgage and living costs and finances the ongoing renovation of the property.

We didn't know much about organising holiday accommodation, but as we'd run hospitality-based companies in the UK, we guessed we knew enough to get by. Before starting work on the house we asked Andrea, our *geometre*, for advice on any Italian regulations governing holiday lets. There were no specified requirements or restrictions for the size of the business we were planning, so we got started on our house renovations.

Preparing for visitors

Work to prepare Casa del Sole for visitors had begun at the end of January. Our rural idyll had been shattered at first light by noisy truck-loads of builders, by the whirr of cement mixers and by a generous layer of mud and dust. Did I care? NO! They were the deliverers of an indoor bathroom and I worshipped them. As the builders toiled away ouside, Richard and I cleaned and decorated indoors. Bursting with plans for the furniture and fittings,

I raided the shops in Pescia and bought everything from linen to extra kettles. My credit card groaned. The advance bookings and 50 per cent deposit I'd accepted from summer guests paid for the necessary extra cookers and fridges. It was the only way we could afford to furnish the house, but it also meant an incredibly tight deadline – we would have to finish renovating by April when the first guests were due to arrive.

At the end of December the olive harvest was over and Richard swapped his olive nets and storage cans for a hammer and saw. Funds were running low and to save money he decided to make some of the furniture needed. Each morning, he scurried to the woodyard with a new diagram scrawled on a scrap of paper. The woodyard owner, Carlo, is old and sun-baked with few remaining teeth; he is always delighted to see us, probably because we provide so much amusement. Presented with Richard's paper, he would squint at the drawing. Turning it this way and that he would finally ask, 'What is it? Is it a door? Is it a staircase? You're

always making the strangest things'. And it's true; Richard has been down there with pictures of windows and doors, beds, staircases, fences, panelling, playground equipment and his most accomplished piece, the 'not quite Californian cold tub', now fully installed on our terrace. They think he is slightly crazy, but Italians admire a man who 'does it himself'. The renovations kept us busy for the first three months of the year, but by April we were ready to receive our first guests.

Far left The chestnut house, ready for guests. Below left Carlo, our woodmerchant. Below Richard's cold tub.

9th April 2003: The guests

After a last minute dash on the day of our guests' arrival, we were finished. Richard went down to the chestnut house to have a final check; disaster, the hot water ran bone-chilling cold. In a panic we rang Daniele, our electrician, who promised to come in the morning. Tonight they would have to bathe in our new bathroom in the farmhouse.

Another problem. The visitors ring to report that one of them has lost her purse – could we pick them up from the airport rather than the station only five minutes away? Richard is dispatched on a rescue mission while I put some dinner in their oven, light their fire and generally try to make up for the fact that the weather has turned sour and is greeting them with rain. They finally arrive in the dark, in high-heeled sandals and with very little luggage. Certainly no warm clothes packed in those bags; I begin to worry.

The next day Richard and I have to visit the hospital in Florence for a scan, which will take all day. The guests are not up when we leave, so I write a note to tell them we'll return later and hope that they're all right. We arrive back at 4pm but they are not at the house. Our plumber thinks they've gone back to Pisa to hire a car, and still it is raining. By 10pm they still haven't returned and I begin to worry; we can't contact them and they haven't rung us. At 1.30am our telephone rings; I dash downstairs but miss the call and there is no message. At 2.30am, again a ring, but no message. Soon after, we notice the chestnut house lights go on. At least they are home safe and sound.

The next day we learn that they'd ventured into town for a meal and then couldn't find their way back. They'd tried to telephone but got no answer. In desperation they rang the police who gallantly escorted them to the end of our driveway; from here they rang again as their escort was convinced there was no house at the end of the road. Again, no answer. They had forgotten the torches we'd provided for night-time navigation so the helpful policeman accompanied them to the house. In the morning we equip them with umbrellas and now they have a car; things are looking up.

Left and below After months of preparation, we began our first season of holiday lets and welcomed guests in April.

Day to Day

BECOMING OFFICIAL: RED TAPE

Managing the guest accommodation, pressing our own olive oil and farming the land means that in Tuscany, as in England, we are self-employed. This limits our contact with bureaucracy to some degree but in Italy, there's really no escaping red tape.

As EU residents we didn't need work permits to establish ourselves in Italy but we did need various other documentation. The most important was the *codice fiscale* (tax code), needed to open a bank account, register with a doctor and to process our *permesso di soggiorno* (residency permit). We discovered that a *codice fiscale* is even needed to pay utility bills and purchase items such as a car.

Applying for a tax code was relatively simple; we just presented the required papers (each region specifies different ones so it's best to check first) at the local tax office and were given a number on the spot. Our application for residency proved to be more complicated. Our *geometre*, Andrea, kindly organised this for us although it was certainly beyond his remit as renovation consultant. It involved sheaves of documents copied in triplicate, filling out numerous forms in Italian and even a trip to the police station. We were told it would take at least three months to process and that we

couldn't buy or insure a car without it. This presented a problem – we'd sold our car in England and now had no transport. We were saved by our friend, Elaine, who bought and insured a car for us in her name while we waited for our residency permits. Not exactly illegal – Italians delight in wriggling around the 'system' – this was a boon but probably not the officially sanctioned route.

Mastering bureaucracy

Italian and English alike had warned us about Italian bureaucracy before our arrival. All the rumours turned out to be true – it is long-winded, pointless and irritates everyone.

After numerous visits to government departments we found that the system mainly involved taking bundles of personal documents to far-flung offices, only to be told that we were in the wrong place, on the wrong day, at the wrong time. Days, even weeks, of time had to be put aside for procedures that should have taken a few hours.

Our two most important lessons were that you will never achieve anything on your first trip to an official and losing your temper gets you nowhere. Italians are used to negotiating knotty bureaucratic spaghetti and take it in their stride. Shouting or openly showing your irritation gains only blank shrugs and referral to the end of another long queue. I found that simply asking for help and saying that I was English and didn't understand the system generally worked as a bit of a fast track. The other sneaky trick was to take Gregory with me – you always have the edge when you brandish a *bambino*.

Negotiating Italian bureaucracy takes time, but tax codes and residency permits were part of establishing ourselves in Italy.

Public money

Recently, on a Friday, I called in at the local builders' merchant to pay our account. It was a large sum and I paid in cash which I'd just withdrawn from the bank. On the following Monday we got a phone call from them that I didn't really understand. Richard went down to the yard to investigate and returned with 50 euros. Apparently I'd overpaid because the banknotes were new and had stuck together. We'd never have known and we were touched by their honesty. We've had similar situations at the woodyard and at a motorway tollbooth where the cashier nearly killed himself leaning out to shout that I'd forgotten my 20 cents change.

On a day-to-day level, we've found that Italians are scrupulously honest about money. When it comes to taxes and public finances, however, another system seems to come into play. As far as I can gather, dodging tax is a national pastime (seemingly endorsed by Prime Minister Berlusconi, who is reputed to have made his millions through tax evasion). There is an endless number of fiddles, culminating in a tax amnesty every few years where you can declare that you owe vast taxes, say you're sorry for not paying (after all, *essere umano* – we're only human), then escape with just 10 per cent of your bill.

Once you've registered for a tax code you are 'in the system' and obliged to submit an annual return. There is no difference (as far as I know) if you are an employee or self-employed. You can compile your own return but given the intricacies of Italian bureaucracy a good accountant is probably a safer option. Income tax in Italy is high – around 40 per cent – and covers pensions, national insurance and government spending. As Richard was working in both the UK and Italy we paid tax in both countries and have been told that we may be able to offset our extra Italian tax against our UK contributions.

Hidden costs

The cost of day-to-day living in Tuscany is much cheaper than in Yorkshire – we spend less on food, on wet weather entertainment, on alcohol, on dining out and on holidays. Some things, however, particularly car insurance and convenience food are much more expensive. Richard is no longer young enough to be classed as a 'boy racer' but the cost of insuring our tiny Renault Clio for six months' third party was the same as a year's fully comprehensive insurance in the UK.

Italian driving habits may be partly to blame. For some reason,

easy-going, casual Italians turn into demons when they get behind the wheel. They overtake on blind bends, only to turn off the road a few yards ahead. Women speed on narrow lanes while chatting on the phone (tucked into their neck), applying lipstick, changing radio channels and buckling children into car seats. Richard gave my mum the best advice I've heard so far: 'Drive carefully, never assume the other car will stop, even if it's your right of way (as the marks on our car prove). If someone hoots they are being friendly; if they flash, you are in their way; if they crash into you, don't worry, it happens to everyone'.

The costs of gas, water and electricity supply are all comparable to the UK, but while heating bills are lower, we sometimes need fans in hot weather. To lower our bills we've installed solar panels to heat our water in summer and use wood from our woodland in winter. Our water is pumped from the stream that runs at the base of our land. For this we pay the local commune a small water rights fee every year, but even with the costs of maintenance and pumping this is cheaper than being supplied from the mains.

House insurance, road tax, personal insurance and pensions are all similar to the UK and equally complicated. We've bent the ears of many new friends asking advice but there are plenty of qualified experts ready to help too.

You need a residency permit to buy and insure a car in Italy. Car insurance is much more expensive than in the UK.

Learning from our experience

FINANCES AND BUREAUCRACY

Relocation involves rethinking careers and working practices and negotiating new bureaucracy. Establishing a new life abroad forced us to reassess and reorganise our work and financial arrangements.

Work

- Don't expect life to be easier just because you are locating to your dream destination. Circumstances and preferences change and while life may be new, exciting and different, it still involves hard work.

- If you are changing career, think carefully about your aptitude for your new job – the weather may be better, but a job you disliked in the UK will not be any more appealing abroad. I'm quite gregarious and enjoy having people around but Richard is more solitary; work-wise, it's best for me to look after the farm guests while Richard manages the land.

- Think through the implications of a lifestyle change – committing yourself to subsistence farming, for example, may mean no holidays, no new clothes and no new car.

- If you plan to continue your career, investigate the local jobs market before you move. Find out whether your qualifications will be recognised and consider whether your language skills are sufficient and if you could be self-employed.

- Take out adequate life insurance. This is even more important in another country than 'at home'. I am amazed at how many English friends haven't taken out insurance in Italy, while in England they would be insured to the hilt. You should at least be covered for the amount of your mortgage and to provide support for any dependents in a worst-case scenario. As Richard does most of the dangerous work on the farm, we've made sure he is well insured, over and above our mortgage cover.

■ Burn your bridges only when you are sure you are safely across. Richard only sold his disco business when we had taken full bookings for the holiday lettings this year and had at least half-filled 2004. Always have an emergency plan in case of financial problems.

Finances

■ Income tax in Italy is around 40 per cent so you will benefit by routing any money you can through the UK. In some circumstances, you may be able to claim back the extra tax paid on your Italian earnings.

■ If you have an income in both Italy and the UK you will have to declare this to both tax authorities. It is helpful to have an accountant in Italy and one in the UK.

■ Tax on house purchases is much lower if you are a first time buyer. To qualify for this you must have a residency permit.

■ Italy lives up to its reputation as a red tape nightmare. Take photocopies of everything in triplicate (including bills, bank statements, mortgage documents, residency confirmation, marriage certificates and birth certificates) whenever you visit government offices. In general, office clerks are happier the more papers you wave at them.

Bureaucracy

■ You will need a *codice fiscale* (tax number) to open a bank account, register with a doctor and process your residency permit. It can be easily obtained from the local tax office.

■ It can take up to three months to process your residency application. This involves the collection and return of forms to the local government commune and registration with the police.

■ You cannot buy or insure an Italian car unless you are a resident. If you bring your car from the UK to use while your residency permit is processed, make sure it is covered by your insurance. We sold our car in England and had to rely on the generosity of a friend to buy and insure an Italian car for us until our permits came through.

Learning from our experience
HEALTH CARE

Italy has an extremely efficient public health-care system which you can access once you are a resident. This doesn't, however, solve the difficulties of explaining medical matters in a new language.

- As an EU citizen you are entitled to use Italy's efficient national health-care system, which includes medical and dental facilities.

- To register with a doctor you will need a *codice fiscale* and a residency permit (see Bureaucracy, page 117).

- It can be useful to obtain copies of your medical records from your UK doctor before relocation.

- Your local government commune can advise on where you should register for health care and the clinic will provide a list of doctors.

- It is important to be able to communicate in health matters. If you are not fluent in Italian, try to find a doctor that can speak at least a little English. Equally, there may not be a translator present if you have to attend hospital; think in advance and establish who you could ask for help in an emergency or if you have a hospital visit or stay.

- It is standard practice for children to visit paediatricians in Italy; the system of registration is the same as for doctors.

- If you want to seek private health care, consultations can be arranged through your national health service practitioner. The public and private systems are more integrated than in the UK.

- Most prescriptions carry a small charge.

Medical system

Once we'd obtained our *codice fiscale* we could register with a doctor. Italy has an extremely efficient public health-care system which, as EU citizens, we were entitled to use, as well as all the usual private facilities. Children register with a paediatrician instead of a regular GP, so Gregory will get more specialist care than in the UK. After much searching I found a female doctor who could speak enough English to match my rudimentary Italian. This became more of an issue when I discovered that I was pregnant. I had an abnormal scan at 20 weeks and found my poor language skills incredibly frustrating. The hospital did all they could to help and found me a translator as well as an English-speaking specialist but it was a reminder that I needed to get back to my grammar books.

Expecting a second baby has made being close to a town with good health-care facilities especially important.

Day to Day

STARTING SCHOOL

A big change for Gregory was starting school in Italy. In England he had attended a nursery while I worked. Now he had to learn a new language as well as make new Italian friends in the playground.

From the age of three Gregory had attended a private nursery for three days a week while I worked. He was learning the alphabet and improving his cognitive skills, but the hours were long for a small boy – 9am to 4pm – and he often came home tired and grumpy.

I hadn't given much thought to schooling before moving to Tuscany. We couldn't afford a private nursery, so I'd assumed Gregory would stay at home until he was four or five and then would start primary school. On arrival, I discovered that children

don't have to attend school until they are six, but can attend a state nursery school affiliated to a primary school from the age of three.

We decided to enrol Gregory for September. My friend Marisa arranged an appointment for us to be shown around the nursery. The children, shrieking in delight in the playground, wore striped pinafores (*grembiuli*), pink for girls, blue for boys. The teachers explained (through Marisa, who interpreted) that the school concentrated on fostering interaction and learning through play. There was less emphasis on rigid, academic learning as numbers, letters and writing, while encouraged in nursery, would be taught in primary school. The children could attend every morning or all day.

First days

We decided that Gregory should only attend school in the mornings; after all, we wanted to spend more time together and didn't want him to feel overwhelmed by new surroundings and a new language. He loved it immediately. In England we had a regular morning battle to get him off to school where he would often cry when I left. Now he cried when I came to pick him up. He wanted to stay for lunch and to play with his new friends. He'd obviously been deprived of young company over the summer and was having great fun with his Italian classmates, even if he didn't know what they were saying.

I eventually gave in when the olive harvest began in November and let him stay all day. Agreeing to the

new hours, his teacher asked me to bring in a blanket and pillow. Thinking I'd misheard, I rang an Italian friend for advice. I'd been right – children have an afternoon siesta at Italian nursery. I eagerly anticipated fewer tired and grumpy outbursts at the end of a hard day at school.

Left A new school uniform. Below Gregory now looks forward to going to school in the morning.

Learning from our experience

EDUCATION

Enrolling at a local school is a good way for children to adjust to new life in a different country and to make friends in the area. Italy offers an excellent state school system for children up to the age of 18 years.

- Children can attend nursery schools affiliated to primary schools from the age of three but this is not compulsory.

- Children must attend primary school from 6 to 11 years of age at the end of which they take an exam – *Licenza elementare*. From 11 to 14 years, children attend *Scuola Media* (middle school), and must pass a final examination. From 14 years children attend Upper secondary school. They must complete the first year after which they can leave at 15 (the end of compulsory education) or continue to complete their diploma at 18.

- Schools are obliged to take all children, regardless of whether they can speak Italian.

- School registration varies from district to district. Ask at the school for the best way to enrol – there is usually a specific week in which you should register.

- Young children tend to pick up language quickly. Attending school with no other English children can help them integrate and make local friends.

- Virtually all primary education is state run, with only a few private schools run by religious groups. Private secondary schools are available but these tend to be specialist schools, such as for dance or drama. International schools are found only in major centres such as Milan, Florence and Rome and tend to be expensive.

School dinners

After enrolling Gregory, I received a letter from school containing a number of menus. There was so much food that I couldn't make head or tail of it. I presumed that they were enquiring whether Gregory had any special dietary needs and had listed what the children might be fed during the year. I took the form back to school saying '*tutto bene*' (it's all good), and didn't think any more about it.

The next month I received a similar letter. By now our Italian lessons were starting to take effect and I could understand a little more. It seemed that the list was actually a four-weekly menu with a different three-course meal for each day. It was my introduction to Italian obsession with good food. Each month the menu changes and, as a parent, you have the right to add dishes or suggest alterations. Schools are even campaigning for their food to be organic and free from genetically modified ingredients. This dedication to the health and welfare of children is seriously impressive. Gregory now eats a *prima* of pasta, a *secondo* of meat and vegetables and a *dolce* (dessert). He's much better fed than we are and unsurprisingly has stopped taking much interest in dinner.

Gregory has quickly adjusted to learning in Italian and now attends school full time.

Italian Life

The Italians have a phrase, 'essere umano'
(to be human), and this seems to be the
guiding principal of life. It can be a get out clause
(as in infidelity) or it can be a kindness (when a
policeman escorts you home because you're lost).
Every day we're surprised by the differences that
'being human' makes in Tuscany. It influences
everything, from how families interact to what
you eat for lunch, to when the shops open.
Sometimes it's frustrating when you're used
to doing things differently, but mostly it's an
opportunity to try something new, to fit in, to
embrace the Italian way and enjoy our new
Tuscan life.

Italian life revolves around the local community and family. Part of fitting in is embracing this way of living.

La familia

Before moving to Tuscany I had a stereotyped idea of the 'Italian family', no doubt fostered by television and too many viewings of *The Godfather*. I thought everyone married young and expected to see plenty of large Italian mammas herding broods of dark-haired children along the streets (part of the reason I didn't worry about my weight gain prior to the move). As it turned out, I was wrong.

I have yet to find the Italian mamma as promoted by numerous bolognese sauce adverts. I'm considered quite overweight here and have already been warned about piling on the kilos during pregnancy as I'm 'very heavy' for my height. Still, I defy anyone to remain stick-thin in a country that prides itself on crumbling almond cakes, bite-tender pasta and whole menus of *gelato*.

Italian women are undeniably, and almost invariably, beautiful. Perfectly manicured, flawlessly made-up and exquisitely dressed, they dedicate a lot of time to their appearance. Sloppy clothes and scruffy shoes are just not permissible. Men, women and children are smart, tailored and crisply pressed at all times. Dressed in my gardening clothes and trailing Gregory in mucky dungarees I used to feel decidedly shabby at the local market on a Saturday morning. I've now slightly modified my dress in deference to our new home, but as the 'mad English' (said with affection) I can usually get away with a few misdemeanours.

Family ties

My other misconception was that Italian families were large. In fact in Italy there is an average of just 0.7 children per couple, while it is 1.9 in the UK. The low birth rate has turned into a national crisis; the Pope has even appeared on national television exhorting all devout Catholics to go forth and procreate. I quizzed Italian friends about falling numbers. Various explanations were given from increased use of the Pill to the fact that Italian boys are so molly-coddled at home they don't want to leave to start their own families. Interestingly,

no one mentioned health matters. In general, Italians smoke like furnaces and drink coffee strong enough to keep me awake for a week. From my experience, this may not be the best way to prepare your body for producing *molti bambini*.

Paradoxically, Italian families are still far larger than those in the UK. Italians consider anyone who is even distantly related to be family. Even cousins twice removed are close family and bonds are incredibly strong. At Christmas we were invited to the house of an Italian friend, Luciano, to see *Babbo Natale* (Father Christmas). Traditionally a local man (in this case a friend of Luciano) dresses up and visits neighbours' homes on Christmas Eve. We were told that family would be there and expected a small group. The house was packed with more than 20 'close relatives'. At our home in England it was viewed with astonishment (and the trepidation associated with a rare and significant event) if we managed to get more than seven relatives in the same room at once.

Making new friends, like Luciano, has made relocation easier and encouraged us to improve our language skills.

Bambini

There may not be many of them, but certainly in Italy, Kids Rule. I worried that all the new attention would turn Gregory into a spoilt brat, but actually the opposite has been true.

Everyone here loves children. Old men drinking and playing cards in a bar will stop to speak to a child and

Girolamo and Susanna run a favourite local restaurant and always stop work to play with Gregory when we visit.

offer sweets. Prams wheeled down the high street are circled by an eager mob anxious to peak at the baby. Women cluck and admire your children, whatever their age. Visiting a playground, Gregory was swept off his feet by two teenage lads who cooed over his blonde hair and invited him to play.

Initially, we were surprised by some of these reactions. In the UK people tend to keep to themselves and no one, but no one, ever touches your child without your permission. Richard and I had a lot of experience of working with children from running the discos. We both love kids and the only work-related thing we miss is the time spent at these events. Yet Richard, more than I, had to be very careful how he treated the children – he made sure he never touched them, not even to dance or to generally play around. I often noticed that parents were too self-conscious, or just not interested, in playing with their kids. It was heart-breaking to see a little boy trying to drag his mummy onto the dance-floor and seeing her refuse. Here in Italy, rough and tumble, playing the fool, getting down to children's level is perfectly acceptable; in fact it is a parental requirement, at home and in public.

A cherished and integrated part of daily life (and usually not too spoiled), children are also welcomed in restaurants and bars. At one of our favourite haunts Gregory is allowed to run around the tables with the owner's grandson, Andrea, while the other diners look on indulgently (in

the UK, 'someone should control that child' would no doubt be muttered in stage whispers). Another restaurant owner, Girolamo, stops work to play as soon as Gregory arrives. They mess around in the garden with Girolamo's dog, a huge Great Dane called Greta; they play marbles on the restaurant floor; they sing together. That Girolamo is about 50 years old and very 'well to do' makes no difference at all.

Fitting in

There is no doubt that we'll always be 'l'inglese' but we do seem to be settling into local community life. Since arriving we've made an effort to be friendly and to try to chat in Italian (usually causing fits of laughter on all sides), but it's really the Italians who have made integration so easy. The general level of friendliness is truly amazing. Visiting a shop to buy some oil canisters, we were invited to dinner so that the owner and his family could practise their English and we our Italian. Numerous dinners later we've become firm friends. This happens all the time. Our electrician invites us for pizza, the lady in the pharmacy advises on bread-making, a neighbour helps to pick olives. It's a fantastic antidote to traditionally English reserve and embraces the fact that friendship is sometimes found in the most unlikely places.

Dipping biscuits into wine is just one local custom we've been introduced to by our new Italian neighbours.

Parlare Italiano

The ease with which we've made friends has been all the more surprising given our poor language skills. We spoke very little Italian on arrival in Tuscany. Richard had taken a few hours of evening classes, but I knew nothing. The first few months were a difficult mixture of confusion, frustration and mistaken purchases.

The process of applying for residency and other documentation was undoubtedly complicated by our lack of Italian, while shopping was more of a lucky dip because we couldn't decipher the labels.

Desperate to improve our skills, we attended lessons for foreigners run by the local government commune and began private lessons as well. The best learning device, however, has been necessity and proximity. As soon as the builders arrived at the farmhouse our Italian improved in leaps. We had to talk to them, so we did. In the same way, Gregory's Italian has been fostered by school. Small children are usually quick to pick up new languages and Gregory has been no exception. A few weeks after enrolling he was already chattering with his new Italian friends and now reminds us that we've certainly got some catching up to do.

Left Organising building work has improved Richard's Italian. Below Gregory has developed his language skills at school.

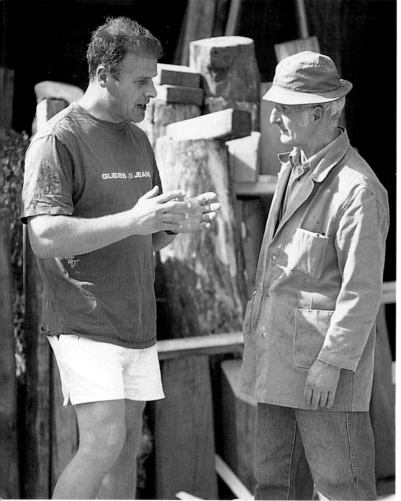

Living healthy

Italian life is good for the soul but it has also been fairly good for the body. Richard and I were members of a gym in England. In fact I used to be an exercise instructor in what now seems like someone else's life. We'd go as often as we could, but being busy this was only once or twice a week – certainly not enough to work off the Yorkshire puddings. I sat at a desk all day, while Richard stood behind his DJ decks. We were getting flabby.

We hoped that moving to Italy would offer a healthier lifestyle with a bit more exercise. *Pronto*! The wish was granted. Our house is up a long, steep track and for most of winter is impassable by car. Carrying all our shopping including a tired child up the slope has provided more than enough exertion. Every day there are also manual jobs to complete on the farm, from digging the potato patch to sweeping the house. Richard gets the least enviable tasks – pushing concrete around in wheelbarrows, felling trees and lifting bricks – but it certainly keeps off the kilos despite delicious Italian food.

The steep track to our house has provided plenty of daily exercise. Moving has meant more of an active, outdoor life.

Italian Life

FOOD

The importance of food cannot be over-estimated in Italy. If children rule then food is Prime Minister. It is an inexhaustible subject discussed by absolutely everybody at every opportunity.

Eating out is a favourite pastime in Italy. When there's time, a long, relaxed lunch is the main meal of the day.

The thing that surprised me most about our builders was their pre-occupation with food. This is not considered a 'girly' topic; it's a very serious matter. In the morning they would discuss recipes and talk about what they were having for lunch; in the afternoon the talk moved to dinner. Every Italian man cooks; he is an expert (although Italians are experts at everything). He knows about ingredients; has detailed knowledge of different cooking methods; he is a food critic. Of course the women are the same but they are usually so slim I can't believe they have first-hand knowledge of the food they're talking about.

Each day breaks down into a serious gourmet ritual. First, breakfast: a *caffé* or perhaps a *cappuccino* and a sweet cake or croissant (the fry-up is a completely alien concept to Italians). Then lunch: if you have time, this is the meal of the day. Ideally it should take about three hours, involve long conversation between courses and at least half a litre of wine. Finally, dinner: lighter than lunch (unless you've had a small one) and eaten very late, around 9pm.

Mangiare

A full Italian meal begins with *antipasti*: a colourful feast of anything bite-sized – small pieces of bread (*crostini*) topped with tiny mounds of tomato, olives or peppers, a selection of peppery salami, salty prosciutto or stuffed olives. Then comes *prima*: a course of pasta or gnocchi, designed to fill you up. Then *seconde*: the meat course of lamb, chicken or beef with vegetables, often potatoes. Finally, *dolce* (pudding). In need of digestive aid, all this is followed by *caffé* and perhaps a fiery grappa.

For a full meal you should be hungry, really hungry – Italians are definitely not into small portions. Richard and I are in heaven. Eating out is generally cheap and the cost of wine (usually the largest part of the bill in the UK) is low due to zero tax. Very few restaurants, however, serve international food and those that do tend to be expensive. People

say, 'Food here is so good, why would I want to try other cuisines?'. I can see their point – Italian food is superb – but I do sometimes hanker for Chinese, Indian and even some English food. I miss fish and chips, but can imagine the Italian verdict on a chip shop: 'Only one type of fish? Only chips? Everything is fried? What is the green mush in this pot? Scraps of what exactly? Where's the wine list? Why can't I smoke in here? I think I'll just have a *caffé*'.

Relaxed meals at home have been inspired by the Italian approach to cooking, eating and socialising.

Vino

Our local area is not as famous as Chianti for wine, but many of our neighbours have their own vineyards and produce fruity reds and lovely lemony whites. Attempts to produce a vintage Casa del Sole wine, however, have proved less of a success.

Our vines were in a very poor state when we first arrived, and unsurprisingly didn't produce many grapes. In fact they bore so little fruit that we pressed the grapes by hand, literally squashing them between our fingers. We then bottled the must and hoped for the best. Lacking any of the right equipment, let alone knowledge, it was really a venture doomed to fail. Still we learned a lot, and this year we've read all we can, looked after our vines and are hoping to produce something at least one step up from 'rough'.

On a scale as small as ours you can't take your grapes to an industrial press. You can, however, try to find a neighbour who makes their own and ask if they'll process your grapes in return for a few bottles (you may want to test a few of their previous vintages first, to make sure that your grapes have been left in safe hands).

Our friend Luciano makes *vin santo* (literally, holy wine), named because a sip is supposed to be like going to heaven. It tastes like sherry and is served with sweet *biscotti* for dunking. Because of its holy name, it seems to be an acceptable tipple at any time of day and we've been plied with it as early as 10am.

Close ties with the land mean that buying wine directly from the vineyard (often your neighbours') or from a wine merchant is commonplace. We buy from Luca, a friend near Montecatini. He buys wholesale, direct from the supplier and can bottle it for you or fill your own can straight from a pump. It's certainly a change from visiting an off-licence.

Below Richard visits our wine supplier Luca to refill our containers. **Right** The vines. **Below right** Our first wine.

To market

As eating is a national pastime, shopping for ingredients is a high priority. Market day in Pescia involves an early start to catch the best of the fresh produce. Spindly plant seedlings, spiny artichokes and golden mounds of apricots sit on the groaning tables.

The market is now so large that it's divided in half: *frutta i verdura* fill the lower square while all manner of bric-à-brac, linen and clothes are sold at the top. As a special Saturday treat, I always pick up a free-range spit-roasted chicken from a bustling stall of blue-aproned vendors. I don't know what they do to the birds, but they are the best chickens I've ever tasted.

My plant man is a familiar face in the bustling sea of stalls. I bought most of my seedlings from him when we first moved to Casa del Sole and never manage to resist a new feathery tomato plant or silvery herb. Bizarrely he always asks about our dogs. I still haven't worked out how he knows about them; perhaps I've got the wrong end of the Italian stick again.

We still visit the local supermarket for the odd item – perhaps washing powder, baking foil or milk – but the fresh market, local shops and our own produce have replaced our weekly Yorkshire superstore trips.

The market provides fresh seasonal ingredients to supplement what we grow in the garden at Casa del Sole.

The kitchen table

Moving to an olive farm has meant new ways of shopping, cooking and eating. Italian food is essentially home cooking and while we eat out more than we did in the UK, we also eat better at home. Busy with work in England, we ate a lot of convenience food and at least two take-away meals a week. Here, there is more time to cook, the ingredients are literally on the doorstep and all the produce is organic.

Each of us has developed our own Tuscan favourites. Gregory has become a pasta tyrant, demanding it at every meal; Richard has developed a taste for toast with mascarpone cheese and chocolate and hazelnut spread (not necessarily healthy but certainly delicious); and I've rediscovered pizza. Some local specialities have proved less popular – a type of tripe, rabbit stew, and strangely the bread, which is made without fat or salt and hardens to an inedible rock after only one day.

Food now follows a seasonal pattern. In spring we might eat beans and artichokes from the garden; in summer tomatoes, cucumbers and courgettes; rhubarb, meaty porcini mushrooms and chestnuts in autumn; and thick bean soups in winter. Four-foot bushes of wild rosemary, swathes of mint, thyme, oregano and sage in the garden mean that fresh herbs are always on hand. Our own free-range eggs have bright sun-orange yolks and taste completely different to those from the shops. Boiled until lightly set, they are now Gregory's breakfast staple.

Of course there are also the olives. No longer a luxury, streams of oil find their way onto bread, salads or pastas, or poured into soups, sauces and even cakes. In the garden there is also the pizza oven. Busy with the house renovations we ignored the small red brick building

Learning new cooking methods has involved mastering the wood-fired pizza oven in the garden at Casa del Sole.

to the side of the house for eight months. Finally, intrigued by its blackened hole, we collected a small pile of wood and initiated the Casa del Sole pizzeria. It was not a success. A mound of branches and twigs must be assembled in the domed heart of the oven. Stoked to a blazing fury they must heat the oven floor to about 400°C. The burning embers are brushed aside, the pizzas then cook in seconds on the superheated stone floor. Our fire was too small, the oven too cold, the dough not mixed with the required Italian skill. Soggy and chewy, the pizzas became dog food.

For our next attempt we called in the experts. Strictly supervised by our wine merchant Luca and his wife Sonia, we rolled out new dough and fired up the oven again. *Bellissimo.* Paper thin, the dough bubbled to a just-crisped round. Olive oil and fresh rosemary from the garden; tomato, basil and mozzarella; and, the most delicious of all, strawberries with a sprinkling of sugar, hot and caramelised in an instant. *Pizza di casa con fragole.* Absolutely divine.

Italian food is 'home cooking'. Dishes are simply prepared using the freshest ingredients and enjoyed together.

Recipes

I've always loved cooking and being able to use home-grown produce has brought a new level of enjoyment. The main point in Italy, whether the ingredients are bought in the market or picked in the garden, is that they are fresh. Pickling and preserving has also become a way to extend the seasons and cope with our summer gluts of fruit and vegetables.

These recipes are my adaptations of dishes from home that have fallen under the Tuscan spell, of food from our favourite restaurants and from local friends who are always on hand to give advice. Italian cooking is not an exact science – I rarely use my measuring scales – experimenting and developing your own themes are all part of the fun.

Bruschetta
Bread brushed with garlic and oil

Locals often celebrate the first oil of the olive harvest with bruschetta. We love it in its simplest form – just doused in Casa del Sole oil. For variation, try a topping of mushrooms or fresh tomato salsa (see page 148).

Serves 6

6 slices stale country-style bread
2 cloves garlic, cut in half
extra virgin olive oil

Toast or grill the bread until light brown. Rub each slice with a cut garlic clove. Douse with olive oil.

Mushroom topping

5 tablespoons extra virgin olive oil
450 g fresh porcini mushrooms, sliced
3 garlic cloves, crushed
1 tablespoon chopped thyme
salt and freshly ground pepper

Heat the oil in a large pan. Add the mushrooms and cook over a high heat for about 5 minutes or until the liquid has evaporated. Add the garlic, thyme and seasoning. Cook for a further minute. Spoon the topping onto the *bruschetta*.

Melanzane alla piastra
Grilled aubergines

Aubergines need lots of sun and thrive in the garden in summer. Brushed with olive oil and grilled, they go well with peppers, basil and mozzarella as part of an antipasto platter or with barbecued or grilled chicken.

Serves 6

3 medium aubergines
2 garlic cloves, crushed
3 tablespoons extra virgin olive oil
salt and freshly ground black pepper

Cut the aubergines into slices lengthways, about 1 cm thick.

Add the garlic to the olive oil. Brush the aubergine with the oil and cook under a preheated hot grill or on a ridged grill pan for 7–8 minutes, brushing with more oil as necessary. Turn once, cooking until tender and golden.

Serve warm or cold.

Carciofi in pinzimonio
Artichokes dipped in oil

Artichokes are a new discovery for us. In spring they fill the local market and appear on the menus of all our favourite restaurants. Small, tender artichokes need no cooking and can be eaten raw as antipasto.

Serves 6

juice of 1 lemon
6 artichokes
6 tablespoons extra virgin olive oil
salt and freshly ground black pepper

Pour the lemon juice into a large bowl of water.

Clean the artichokes, discarding the stem and the tough outer leaves.

Cut each artichoke in half, lengthwise, and remove the furry inner choke with a sharp knife. Drop the artichokes into the bowl of water to prevent them discolouring. Drain and pat dry. Arrange on a dish.

Place the oil in a small bowl and add salt and pepper to taste. Eat the artichokes by dipping the leaves one by one into the oil.

Insalata caprese
Salad of sliced tomatoes, basil and mozzarella

We eat this dish every day in summer, taking advantage of my abundant tomato crop. Finding the ripest, juiciest tomatoes and the freshest mozzarella are the key to producing the perfect salad.

Serves 6

3 large mozzarella balls (preferably buffalo)
8 ripe tomatoes
large bunch fresh basil
oregano, fresh or dried
extra virgin olive oil
balsamic vinegar
crusty bread, to serve

Slice the tomatoes, pouring off any excess juice. Cut the mozzarella into slices. Remove the large stalks from the basil.

Arrange the basil, cheese and tomatoes on a plate (in this order, if you're being nationalistic, to match the Italian flag). Sprinkle on a little oregano. Drizzle with olive oil and add a dash of balsamic vinegar.

Serve with crusty bread.

Facioli in umido
Tuscan baked beans

I can't find baked beans in Tuscany so I've made up my own recipe to keep Gregory happy.

Serves 6

800 g tinned cannellini beans or 340 g dried beans
10 tomatoes, finely chopped or 800 g tinned chopped tomatoes
2 leeks (or 2 red onions, if you prefer)
passata
extra virgin olive oil
4 teaspoons brown sugar
salt and freshly ground black pepper
crusty bread, to serve

If using tinned beans, just rinse in cold water. If using dried beans, soak in cold water overnight, then drain.

Preheat oven to 160°C. Put beans, chopped tomatoes (skin or no skin, depending on how rustic you feel), leek or onion and a good slug of olive oil into an ovenproof dish with a lid. Pour over enough passata to cover. Add the sugar, and salt and pepper to taste.

Place the beans in the oven for 20 minutes then remove and stir to stop them burning on the sides. Taste for seasoning and add more if needed. Return to the oven for a further 30 minutes or until soft.

Remove from the oven and serve with crusty bread. The beans freeze well and can also be bottled.

Patate al forno al rosmarino
Roast potatoes with rosemary

This recipe evokes the delicious smells of Tuscany as it cooks and the potatoes taste divine.

Serves 6

6 large potatoes (preferably floury)
extra virgin olive oil
sea salt
sprigs of fresh rosemary

Preheat oven to 200°C. Peel potatoes and chop into large chunks.

Take a large roasting dish, pour in enough olive oil to cover the base, then add the same amount again. Place the dish in the oven until the oil is heated.

When hot, add the potatoes and toss in the oil, ensuring they are well covered. Sprinkle on a generous amount of salt. Lay the rosemary sprigs on top of the potatoes.

Return the dish to the oven, removing after 30 minutes and then every 15 minutes to turn the potatoes. Bake for at least 50 minutes or until golden with crispy edges.

Ragù
Meat and tomato sauce

Ragù, or Ragù Bolognese, is a general term for a meat sauce. It's fantastically useful for any type of pasta.

Serves 6

1 tablespoon extra virgin olive oil
1 onion, finely chopped
1 celery stick, finely chopped
1 carrot, finely chopped
50 g pancetta (or bacon), finely chopped
500 g minced beef or pork
1 beef stock cube
1 tablespoon of plain flour
150 ml dry white or red wine
400 g tinned chopped tomatoes
1 bay leaf
2 tablespoons passata
pinch dried oregano
pinch grated nutmeg
salt and freshly ground black pepper

In a large saucepan, heat the oil and gently fry the onion, celery, carrot and pancetta for about 6 minutes, stirring frequently, until the onion is softened.

Add the beef and cook until coloured. Crumble in the stock cube and add the flour, stir well. Add the wine and boil until mostly evaporated. Add the tomatoes, bay leaf, passata, oregano, nutmeg and seasoning.

Cook, covered, over a low heat for about 1 hour, stirring every 15 minutes. Add a little water if the sauce becomes too dry. Remove bay leaf to serve.

Lasagne al forno
Lasagne

The best thing about this dish is that once it's in the oven (al forno), you can put your feet up. It makes a great family meal served with a rocket salad.

Serves 6

1 quantity ragù sauce (see left)
9 lasagne sheets (no pre-cook)
2 tablespoons freshly grated Parmesan cheese

Béchamel sauce

50 g butter
50 g plain flour
500 ml milk
pinch grated nutmeg
salt and freshly ground pepper

Prepare the ragù. Preheat the oven to 180ºC. While this ragù is simmering make the béchamel sauce.

Melt the butter in a small pan. Add the flour a little at a time, stirring continuously. Cook, stirring, for 1–2 minutes. Remove the pan from the heat and gradually stir in the milk, a little a time. Mix well to ensure there are no lumps. Add nutmeg and seasoning. Return the pan to the heat and cook, stirring continuously, until the sauce is smooth and thick (about 5 minutes). If the sauce is too thick, you can add a little more milk.

Spoon a layer of the ragù over the base of a lightly greased ovenproof dish. Cover with a layer of lasagne. Continue with a layer of ragù, then béchamel, then lasagne. Repeat the layers, finishing with a layer of béchamel sauce.

Sprinkle with freshly grated Parmesan cheese and a grating of nutmeg. Place on a tray in the oven to catch any drips. Bake for about 40 minutes until golden brown on top and bubbling. Remove from the oven and allow to stand for 10 minutes before serving.

Fusilli alla carbonara
Pasta with carbonara sauce

Gregory's spaghetti-handling skills still need a bit of refinement, so instead of making traditional spaghetti alla carbonara, I use fusilli instead. The sauce is lovely and creamy and works best if you make it with proper Italian pancetta.

Serves 6

500 g dried fusilli
1 tablespoon extra virgin olive oil
250 g pancetta, cut into small cubes
300 ml milk
6 egg yolks
50 g freshly grated Parmesan cheese, plus extra to serve
salt and freshly ground black pepper

Bring a large pan of salted water to the boil. Add the pasta and cook until *al dente* (bite tender).

Meanwhile, heat the oil in a frying pan and cook the pancetta over a medium heat, stirring frequently until it is brown and crisp. Remove from the heat and pour off any excess fat.

In a bowl mix together the egg yolks and milk. When the pancetta has cooled, add it to the egg mixture.

Drain the pasta, return it to the saucepan and pour in the egg mixture, Parmesan and seasoning. Toss together – the heat from the pasta should cook the eggs enough to form a coating.

Serve immediately with an extra sprinkling of Parmesan and a fresh green salad.

Pollo alle erbe
Herbed chicken

Chopped fresh herbs give this easy roast dinner a seasonal flavour. In winter I use rosemary or thyme; in summer I use basil or tarragon, depending on which is flourishing in the garden.

Serves 6

1 chicken, about 1.8 kg
90 g butter
3 cloves garlic, peeled and finely chopped
large handful fresh herbs, finely chopped
salt and freshly ground black pepper
150 ml dry white wine

Preheat the oven to 220ºC. Place the chicken in a roasting tin. Mash the garlic into the butter. Mix in the herbs and seasoning.

Smear the herb butter all over the chicken, inside and out. Pour the wine into the roasting tin around the chicken. Cook in the oven for 15 minutes, then lower the heat to 190ºC for a further 40 minutes. Baste the chicken with the pan juices from time to time; add a little more wine or some water if it is becoming dry.

Turn off the oven and allow the chicken to rest for 10 minutes before carving. Serve with the juices from the roasting tin.

Zabaione
Sweet custard

We eat this heavenly custard with fresh fruit in summer, poured over cakes or best of all, just by itself. It's a great way to use up the surplus eggs from our chickens and bears no relation to the floury packet custard we ate before coming to Tuscany.

6 egg yolks
3 tablespoons caster sugar
125 ml sweet Marsala
250 ml double cream

Place the egg yolks and sugar in a heatproof bowl on top of a pan of warm water. Start whisking the yolks and sugar as the water begins to simmer. The mixture should begin to thicken and increase.

Add the Marsala very slowly and whisk for a further 5 minutes, or until the mixture is starting to hold its shape.

In a large bowl, whisk the cream until it forms soft peaks. Gently fold in the egg and Marsala mixture.

Pour the mixture into individual glasses or bowls. Cover and refrigerate for 2–3 hours before serving.

Fragole con aceto balsamico
Strawberries and balsamic vinegar

Wild strawberries grow all over the hills and roadsides during summer. Fruit and vinegar may sound like a strange mix but once you've tried it, you'll be hooked (if you haven't eaten your berries on the way home).

mascarpone cheese
icing sugar
strawberries
balsamic vinegar
freshly ground black pepper

Sweeten the mascarpone cheese, to taste, with the icing sugar and place in a serving bowl.

Rinse the strawberries and pat dry. Place in a large bowl or individual glasses and sprinkle with balsamic vinegar. Add a couple of grinds of black pepper.

To eat, dunk the strawberries in the mascarpone and pop them in your mouth. Delicious.

Biscotti da vin
Home-made biscuits for wine

*Our neighbour Luciano makes vin santo, a divinely
sweet dessert wine. It's a Tuscan tradition to serve this
with small almond biscuits for dipping, so I regularly
bake a batch, with Gregory helping to roll the dough.*

Makes about 48 biscuits

250 g plain flour
$^1/_2$ teaspoon baking powder
180 g caster sugar
pinch salt
90 g almonds, finely chopped
zest of $^1/_2$ lemon
juice of $^1/_2$ lemon
2 eggs
butter, for greasing

Preheat the oven to 180ºC. In a large bowl mix the
flour, sugar, salt and almonds. Now add the lemon
zest, lemon juice and eggs.

Mix together to form a sticky dough. On a lightly
floured surface, divide the dough into fist-sized balls
and roll into log shapes about 20 cm long. Place the
strips on a greased baking sheet about 5 cm apart and
bake for 20 minutes or until golden brown.

Remove from the oven and make diagonal cuts across
each log to form biscuits about 2 cm thick. Return to
the oven for 10 minutes.

Allow to cool. Eat, dipped in *vin santo.*

Pizza di casa con fragole
Casa del Sole strawberry pizza

*Our friends Silvia and Luca taught us how to use the
pizza oven at Casa del Sole and introduced us to this
local recipe. The hot oven intensifies the flavour of the
strawberries and the caramelised sugar gives an
irresistible crunch. It's become a house speciality.*

Serves 6

15 g fresh yeast
$^1/_2$ teaspoon caster sugar
150 ml lukewarm water
300 g strong white flour, plus extra for dusting
1 heaped teaspoon salt
1 tablespoon extra virgin olive oil

400 g strawberries, hulled and sliced
3 tablespoons caster sugar

Preheat the oven to 200ºC. Place the yeast and sugar
in a cup with a little of the water. Leave to dissolve for
about 10 minutes.

Place the flour and salt in a large bowl, make a well in
the centre and pour in the yeast mixture. Using a fork,
mix with circular movements to bring the flour into the
liquid. Add the remaining water and olive oil and mix
to form a moist dough.

Transfer the dough to a lightly floured work surface
and knead for 8–10 minutes. Form the dough into a
ball, make an incision in the top, and place in a lightly
floured bowl. Cover with cling film and leave to rise in
a warm, dry place until doubled in size (1–3 hours).

Knock back the dough, knead for 2–3 minutes and
divide into 6 portions. Flatten the balls with your hand
and use a rolling pin to make circles about 2.5 mm
thick. Transfer to a lightly floured baking sheet.

Top the pizzas with the strawberries and a good
sprinkling of sugar. Cook in the oven for about
10 minutes until the sugar has caramelised and the
pizzas are crisp.

Passata
Concentrated tomato sauce

Passata means 'puréed' and refers to a concentrated sauce of pulped tomatoes. A store-cupboard staple for pasta and pizzas, the beauty of making your own is that you can add herbs, chilli, garlic or onion to taste.

ripe tomatoes
large pinch of salt

Peel the tomatoes by scoring them from top to bottom with a sharp knife then plunging them into boiling water for about 1 minute to loosen the skins. Drain the tomatoes and peel.

Whizz the tomatoes in a food processor until pulped or push through a mincer. Pass the pulp through a sieve to remove the pips.

Transfer to a pan on the hob, add the salt and bring to the boil. Allow to simmer rapidly for about 30 minutes until reduced to the required consistency – the longer you cook the tomatoes, the thicker the sauce becomes.

Allow to cool. Use immediately or transfer to sterilised jars or bottles (see Hints & Tips, page 159) and seal.

Once bottled, the *passata* will keep for up to 1 year in a cool, dark place.

Variations

If you want to include other ingredients in your *passata* such as herbs, chilli, onions or garlic, add them to the tomatoes at the cooking stage.

Salsa alla crudaiola
Fresh tomato salsa

This tomato salsa makes a great dip or topping for bruschetta (see page 148). It also works well tossed through hot pasta, or with barbecued chicken or fish.

500 g ripe tomatoes
1 garlic clove, finely chopped
2 small shallots or spring onions, finely chopped
large handful basil leaves, roughly torn
2 tablespoons extra virgin olive oil
salt and freshly ground black pepper

Peel the tomatoes (see *Passata*, left). Cut the tomatoes in half, deseed, then chop them finely.

Mix all the ingredients together. Leave at room temperature for about 30 minutes to marinate. The salsa will keep in the refrigerator for a couple of days.

Variations

For a hotter salsa, replace the basil with chopped parsley and add 1–2 red chillies, deseeded and finely chopped (or dried chilli flakes, to taste). For a more piquant salsa replace the shallots with 1 tablespoon of chopped capers or chopped olives and three finely chopped anchovy fillets.

Chutney di giardiniere
Garden chutney

I make chutney out of anything there is a glut of in the garden. The secret is to get a balance of sweet and sour flavours, so I always combine sweet fruit with vegetables. You can also add any spices, herbs or even dried fruit you fancy; I've never made the same chutney twice. The following amounts are only a guide – vary the salt and sugar levels according to taste and your chosen ingredients. You can experiment until you get a flavour you like. The method is the same, regardless of quantity.

4 kg fruit and vegetables, chopped finely
1 litre red or white wine vinegar
750 g light soft brown sugar, or to taste
1 teaspoon salt, or to taste
selected herbs and spices

Place any hard ingredients (such as apples, carrots or onions) in a large, heavy-bottomed saucepan with a little water and let them 'sweat' for about 5 minutes to soften. Add soft ingredients (such as peaches, apricots or tomatoes) to the pan. Mince any garlic or ginger and finely chop any herbs; add to the pan with chosen spices. Add salt and brown sugar, adjusting quantities to taste.

Pour in the vinegar; it should just cover the ingredients. Simmer gently for 1–2 hours, stirring occasionally to ensure the chutney doesn't stick. The chutney is ready when it is the consistency of thick jam and there is no residual liquid. Leave to cool for 10 minutes then pour into hot, sterilised jars (see Hints & Tips, right).

Verdure miste sott'olio
Mixed preserved vegetables

Finding a way to preserve some of my vegetable harvest was the only way to prevent it going to waste. It's also a lovely way of extending the tastes of the summer into the winter months.

400 g courgettes
400 g aubergines
400 g red and yellow peppers
150 g salt
800 ml white wine vinegar
3 cloves garlic, peeled and thinly sliced
6 fresh bay leaves
6 sprigs each thyme and rosemary
15 black peppercorns
250 ml olive oil

Cut the aubergines and courgettes lengthways into thin strips. Cut the peppers in half lengthways, core and deseed, then cut into strips about the same size as the other vegetables.

Take a large plastic container and layer the vegetables, sprinkling a good handful of salt between the layers and ending with a sprinkling of salt. Cover the vegetables with a plate, place a weight on top and set aside for about 2 hours in a cool place.

The vegetables should exude a lot of liquid. Pour off the liquid and squeeze out the excess. Pour on the vinegar and leave for 2 hours.

Drain the vegetables, squeeze out the excess liquid and place in a bowl with the garlic, bay leaves, herbs, peppercorns and olive oil. Mix well, then transfer to sterilised jars (see Hints & Tips, right). Leave for a few days before using. They will keep for up to 6 months.

Marmellata della mora
Blackberry jam

Jam making is great fun and a good excuse to go fruit picking. My jam recipe from Yorkshire has been put to good use in Italy with the abundant summer berries.

2 kg blackberrries
2 kg jam sugar (with added pectin)
juice of 2 lemons

Place 4 saucers in the coldest part of the refrigerator.

Pick over the fruits, removing any leaves and stalks. (There is no need to wash the berries; the cooking will purify them.) Place the fruit, sugar and lemon juice in a preserving pan (or large, heavy-bottomed, stainless steel pan) over a low heat and let the sugar dissolve and the fruit soften. As the juices begin to run, gently stir the fruit to ensure the sugar is fully dissolved.

Once the sugar is dissolved, turn up the heat and bring the jam to the boil. Boil hard for 7 minutes then test for setting point. To test for set, remove the pan from the heat. Spoon a little jam onto a chilled plate. Let it cool and push it with your fingertip; the surface should form a crinkly skin. If not, return the pan to the heat and boil for a further 4 minutes. Repeat the test until setting point is reached.

Remove the pan from the heat and allow the jam to cool for about 10 minutes then pour into warm, dry sterilised jars (see Hints & Tips, right). Seal immediately with wax discs and cover with cellophane or a screw-top lid. Label when cool.

Hints & Tips
How to sterilise jars

Sterilising your jars before filling them with pickled vegetables, chutney or jams, is essential to ensure that the contents remain free from bacteria and mould.

To sterilise jars, wash them thoroughly in hot soapy water, rinse them in warm water, then dry with a clean towel. Now place them in a moderate oven (180°C) for at least 5 minutes. Always fill the jars while they are still hot.

Hints & Tips
How to bottle

Bottling is actually very easy and a good way of saving space in the freezer. Last year I bottled kilos of vegetables and fruits as well as pan loads of passata. The best jars to use are those with 'safety dimple' lids.

To bottle sauces

Cook your sauce as usual then transfer into sterilised jars with the lids on but not sealed. Place the jars in a large pan of cold water – the water should come about half-way up the jars. Bring the water to the boil and allow to bubble for about 30 minutes.

Remove the jars from the water, carefully screw down the tops and leave to cool. The dimple on the tops of the jars will be sucked in if they are properly sealed. If the jars are not properly sealed, you can still freeze the sauce or eat it immediately.

To bottle tomatoes

Peel the tomatoes (see *Passata*, page 156). Boil enough water to cover the tomatoes in the jar then add 2 dessertspoons of salt per ½ litre of water. Pack the tomatoes tightly in the jars (you can also add some basil leaves) and pour in the salted water to cover. Bottle as above.

The Future

One thing I've learned from our move is never to try to predict the future. Our lives have always relied heavily on chance, but we've made the most of whatever opportunities have swept past. This doesn't make us feel insecure; Richard and I know that we are ultimately responsible for our own decisions and choices. This is the ethos that has brought us to Casa del Sole and I'm fairly certain that we'll be here a good long while. We've gained so much knowledge and enjoyment

in the last few months that we can only feel optimistic about life ahead. Of course things go wrong, but we've weathered enough storms to hope that we'll overcome the obstacles.

Our next big challenges are the consolidation of our holiday lets and the birth of our new son, due in July. Autumn will bring another

olive harvest as well as the need for repairs to the house. We should be better prepared for the olives this time, with more helpers and more nets. In January we hope to start selling our oil. The olives will need pruning in February and, if the oil sells well, we may finally be able to renovate our side of the farmhouse. March will see us preparing for the year's new guests and I will be buying two piglets and having my first taste of 'pork rearing'. The cycle begins again. The garden will have to be tended throughout and at some point we'll have to tackle the jungle of our woodland.

We've been through so much, worked so hard and become so settled here that it seems inconceivable we were in the UK in our old house and old jobs only a year ago. Casa del Sole is now home and we're both agreed, we don't want to go back.

Acknowledgements

A big thank you to my best friend Kirsty Gibson for organising just about everything to do with this book and for still remaining loyal after the most hectic weeks of both of our lives. Special thanks to Anna Cheifetz, my editor, who has more patience and better ideas than I could ever lay claim to. Huge thanks also to our photographer Ben, for his inspired vision and to our designer Emma, who has done a fabulous job while still managing to get married in the middle of this project. I am also grateful to Polly Powell at Cassell Illustrated for giving the book unwavering support and to the team at Ricochet who filmed the series *No Going Back* and *Tuscan Living*. Particularly Billy Paulet, who puts up with our whims, and our producer, Suzanne Lynch, who always brings fun. Finally, thank you to Richard, who is my rock; I love you beyond reason. And Gregory, whom I have every reason to adore. Also, here's thanks to the Italian people, who have made us so welcome and inspired us in so many ways.

Useful addresses:
Rental villas and property: www.tastethesun.com
Tourist offices: www.towd.com
Moving: www.monstermoving.com
UK tax issues: www.inlandrevenue.gov.uk
Pets abroad: www.defra.gov.uk
Kids abroad: www.travellingwithchildren.co.uk
Mums abroad: www.mumsnet.com or www.bumpsmaternity.com
Alternative technology: www.cat.org.uk